I Remember
BEN HOGAN

I Remember
BEN HOGAN

*Personal Recollections and Revelations
of Golf's Most Fascinating Legend
from the People Who
Knew Him Best*

MIKE TOWLE

**Cumberland House
Nashville, Tennessee**

Published by Cumberland House Publishing, Inc.

Cover design by Gore Studio, Inc.
Cover photo by Jules Alexander
Text design by Mary Sanford

Library of Congress Cataloging-in-Publication Data
Towle, Mike.

   I remember Ben Hogan : personal recollections and revelations of golf's most fascinating legend from the people who knew him best / Mike Towle.
      p. cm.
   Includes index.
   ISBN 978-1-63026-993-7
      1. Hogan, Ben, 1912--Anecdotes. 2. Golfers--United States--Anecdotes.
I. Title.

GV964.H6 T69 2000
796.352'092--dc21
[B]

                                                        99-059625
978-1-58182-078-2 (hc)

To Nanny and Roy Carpenter,
and Grandma and Grandpa Towle;
the most wonderful grandparents a person could have

Contents

ACKNOWLEDGMENTS

Many people made this book possible by consenting to interviews, including a number of Ben Hogan confidants and cronies who have long been reluctant to talk on the record about a man they loved and admired. Thanks to all of you for being forthcoming: Al Geiberger, John Mahaffey, George Archer, Charles Coody, Bruce Fleisher, Hale Irwin, John Jacobs, Rocky Thompson, Kermit Zarley, Lee Trevino, Jim Ferree, Bob Charles, Mason Rudolph, Gene Littler, Gary McCord, Ken Venturi, Kris Tschetter, Tom Byrum, Joel Edwards, Tommy Jacobs, Lionel Hebert, Johnny Pott, Jack Tooke, Jacqueline Hogan Towery, W. A. "Tex" Moncrief, Bob Wynne, Mike Wright, Galyn Wilkins, Marty Leonard, Gene Smyers, Charlie Hudson, Dr. Jim Murphy, Doxie Williams, Jerry Austry, Tim Scott, and Dee Kelly.

Jacqueline Hogan Towery went the extra mile, allowing me to use a number of wonderful photos from her family scrapbook, and those photos added a lot to this book. I also give an extra thanks to Tim Scott for sharing with me a Hogan story included in his own book about Hogan that he is writing.

Jules Alexander was outstanding, as usual, in providing his terrific photography. Thomas Gilbert at AP/Wide World Photos also came through in the clutch.

Ron Pitkin, Cumberland House publisher, showed a willingness and enthusiasm to break into the golf genre of books with this project. My editor, Mary Sanford, brought a nice touch in giving this book the polish it needed and deserved. Ed Curtis was always a patient sounding board during the process of putting this book together.

Curt Sampson, a wonderful writer and good pal, gave me a whole new level of appreciation and admiration for Ben Hogan while I tagged along as editor on his book *Hogan*. Tom Bast helped me brainstorm the idea that became the basis for this book.

My wife, Holley, and my son, Andrew, patiently and cheerfully stood by for many hours while I locked myself away and labored to put this book together.

I thank our Lord, Jesus Christ, for His divine blessings and protection.

INTRODUCTION

Actually, Ben Hogan needs no introduction.

One thing we know: Few people really knew Hogan. But a few hundred million know of him. If they don't know about him from the memorable, Hogan-out-of-hiding television commercials he did in the late 1980s touting his namesake company's new Edge clubs, they are at least familiar with his place in golf history. Two Masters titles. A British Open victory in his only try. Four U.S. Open titles (or was it actually five as he claimed?). The epic association—not friendship, really—with fellow Fort Worth–area native Byron Nelson. Three major victories in 1953, then skipping the fourth. Shooting a 66 at Augusta at age fifty-four. Shooting a 64 at Shady Oaks when he was sixty-five.

We know that his dad, Chester Hogan, committed suicide when Ben was nine, and it is speculated that little Ben was in the same room when Chester pulled the trigger. We know that

Hogan made himself great by digging his game out of the ground. Then there was the Greyhound Bus collision with his Cadillac. *Follow the Sun. Five Lessons.* The Secret. The Slammer. The Hogan Company. "Mr. Dunlop." The yips. The Venturi interview. The daily roundtable at Shady Oaks Country Club. His 1997 funeral.

Valerie.

The most popular image of Hogan is of him hidden from the spotlight: tightlipped and reserved in his days as a golf champion; tightly wound recluse in his retirement days, supposedly ready to bark at the first stray reporter or curiosity seeker who crossed his path. To think of Hogan that way, however, is to take the easy way out, and that's something Hogan never did in any aspect of his life, whether it be golf, making golf clubs, drilling for oil, or penning a best-selling instructional. Damn the public perception: Hogan was actually a shy man with a big heart, although he didn't suffer fools well. He abhorred the company of blabbermouths, yet he was known to pepper friends he respected with penetrating questions on subjects other than golf. Children and dogs, he loved. Outdoor walks and analytical discussions of the golf swing, he adored. If he read of a stranger or child with a grave illness or debilitating injury, he wouldn't hesitate to write a check and mail it, no questions asked.

Friends? The Hogans had friends, and they entertained, and then they went out when those friends reciprocated. Hogan and Valerie broke bread and raised toasts of wines while socializing with friends, and they both adhered to high-class societal rules of etiquette with the strictest of standards. Hogan, a recluse? Perhaps. But sometimes it couldn't hurt to ask to see him. That's what I did in April 1989, when I was doing a story on the yips for the *Fort Worth Star-Telegram*. I approached Hogan, realizing he might have been a yipster for the ages. Two weeks after I made my interview request, and a week after my Hogan-less story ran, I got a call back from Hogan's assistant, Doxie Williams, telling me Mr. Hogan had consented to an interview with a stranger, me, something he hadn't done with any other print reporter in something like ten years.

I asked for twenty minutes; he gave me forty-five. First, there was the handshake: It was firm and powerful—a seventy-six-year-old man one squeeze away from making a man less than half his age cry uncle. It was a gracious three-quarters of an hour, but an uncomfortable one. Questions written on a notepad didn't help: His answers were a complete sentence at best, and the cold stare from behind his huge desk locked his eyes on mine, and quickly I found myself not daring to glance at my pad. (I don't know what color Hogan's eyes were—I tend not to notice those things; one story in this book says "gray," another says "blue.") When it was over, he walked me to his office door, bid me adieu, and then "reminded" me that he was supposed to read the article before it was published. Newspaper ethics don't allow that, and the only concession my editor was willing to make was to let Hogan read only those portions that contained his quotes. I don't think Hogan ever got to see any of the story before it ran, and I never asked.

Hogan didn't really have the yips, you know. At least he didn't show the classic symptoms as discussed in an eighties' study of the yips funded in part by Mac O'Grady and Gary McCord, two of golf's classic anti-Hogans. Golfers with the yips typically jerk the putter on short putts, occasionally knocking a five-foot putt ten feet past the cup. Hogan performed his fair share of that scary stuff, but his putting problems went beyond a simple involuntary twitch or jerk. Some of his twenty-foot putts made it only halfway to the hole, and that's when he was able to get his putter back. Hale Irwin remembers being horrified as a fifteen-year-old while watching

Hogan freeze over a putt at the 1960 U.S. Open at Cherry Hills. It went through Irwin's mind at the time that a bird might land on Hogan's head, and Irwin isn't laughing when he tells the story.

I remember Ben Hogan from another occasion, this also from my days with the *Fort Worth Star-Telegram*. The Fort Worth Chamber of Commerce was putting on a ceremony to introduce its inaugural class of inductees for the Fort Worth Sports Hall of Fame. Hogan was there, of course. Byron Nelson, too. At an opportune time, I asked them to step aside from the madding crowd so I could stand between them for a photo; Nelson and Hogan in their nicely posed smiles, and me in my inch-long flattop, à la Arnold Schwarzenegger's commando. I sent the framed photo to my grandfather as a Christmas gift. Word eventually came back to me from an uncle that my golf-savvy grandfather knew the man on the left and recognized the gent on the right, but he had had to ask who the guy in the middle was. So much for the flattop, although Hogan loved it. He detested long hair and hippies.

I Remember Ben Hogan isn't a biography in the traditional sense of being a chronology wrapped around an author's interpretation and analyses of people, places, things, and events. For that, you would be better served reading Curt Sampson's fascinating *Hogan*. Instead, this is more of an oral history, filled with isolated anecdotes, remembrances, and insights presented in the first person by dozens of people who knew Hogan at one level or another. The list includes professional golfers from Hogan's era, active tour pros, Fort Worth friends and confidants from Hogan's inner circle, fellow Shady Oaks Country Club members, and many others including his personal physician, longtime office secretary, and closest surviving relative.

Some of what is presented in this book is mildly revelatory, and all of it certainly offers fresh perspective and insights into Hogan. There was little attempt made on my part to either decipher what is included, to formulate subjective conclusions, or to dig any deeper when red flags were raised. Many of the sources quoted in this book were reluctant to contribute and did so only when assured I wasn't out to dig dirt on Hogan. I believe the tradeoff was well worth it and that you will find this a rich source of material that allows you to know Hogan better than ever before.

Let me reintroduce you to Ben Hogan.

—*Mike Towle*

I Remember
BEN HOGAN

Hogan, the Man (and His Wife)

He could not tolerate a hippie-style person at all. If you didn't have a good, short haircut, he was ticked.

—Dr. Jim Murphy
Hogan's personal physician

There were two sides to Ben Hogan: Hogan Heavy and Hogan Lite. The former could reduce confident people to shrinking violets; the latter possessed a feathery touch as delicate as a flop wedge out of the second cut of rough behind a green sloping away. Hogan Lite had a dry sense of humor, and it was at work more than listeners realized. At times, Hogan was the epitome of someone best understood if you listened to what he said, not how he said it. Even his humor was often couched in gruff tones.

Wild and crazy for Hogan Lite was driving fishing buddy Earl Baldridge's big Cadillac (at Hogan's insistence) and getting pulled over for speeding outside Dallas. Just for fun and a bit of tease, he sometimes introduced himself as "Hennie Bogan." Transposing the initials of one's name is an age-old act of intentional silliness, although for Hogan it simply was a way to sidestep a lifelong bout of shyness. This was "the Wee Icemon" breaking the ice.

Hogan Lite had a heart. When a Shady Oaks Country Club grill employee was hospitalized after being shot during a robbery across town, Hogan passed the hat among club members and raked in nearly seven thousand dollars as a gift for the young woman. When dogs showed up at the clubhouse door, Hogan was the one bearing a gift slab of steak or hamburger patty. Grownups playing golf at Shady Oaks rarely got so much as a glimpse from Hogan, but show up with a towheaded kid bearing a Tom Watson smile, and Hogan was putty in his hands.

The Hawk?

The Dove.

Common to the multidimensional Hogan was his ability to mesmerize, as well as his attention to detail. No Boy Scout was better prepared than Hogan. Unlike most men of his era—or any other generation for that matter—Hogan preferred button-down pants to ones with zipper. It wasn't a fashion statement; it was the efficiency expert at work. Ben liked the buttons because zippers could stick at inopportune times—up when he needed to take a leak in the middle of a round; down after exiting a port-o-john. Golf history would have been forever changed had Hogan gone through a round with his fly down. It wasn't going to happen.

Most professional golfers without the nickname "Volcano" don't get easily rattled. Tell them, however, that an introduction to Hogan is imminent, and watch knees turn to cookie dough.

Joel Edwards, a veteran tour golfer and long-time resident of the Dallas–Fort Worth area, was thrilled—and scared stiff—when he finally got to shake hands with Hogan:

Mike Tschetter, a friend of mine and fellow golfer who knew Hogan, knew I was a Hogan nut, and being from the Fort Worth–Dallas area I had always wanted to meet the man. One day Mike calls me up and says, "Joel, we're

Hogan tries to relax while contemplating a putt in the second round of the 1953 U.S. Open at Oakmont. Hogan went on to win, giving him the second of three major tournament titles he won that year. (AP/Wide World Photos)

7

playing Shady Oaks tomorrow, and, yes, he's going to be there." Sure enough, we get there, it's about eleven o'clock, and I'm going, "He's not going to show, he's not going to show, he's not going to show." And Mike goes, "Don't worry. He'll be here at 11:30, right on the dot." And at 11:25, I'm going, "He's not going to show, he's not going to show," and I'm shaking. Then right at 11:30, he comes walking through the door, and I'm in awe. He walks up to Mike. Mike stands up and I stand up, but he never looks at me. He looks straight into Mike's eyes, something I'll never forget, and says, "Mike, how are you doing? Are you playing all right? How you hittin' it?" Just the same ol' stuff a friend would ask you, but here's *Ben Hogan* asking the same questions.

He never looked at me, even though when you meet people you normally see other people around them. Finally Mike says, "Mr. Hogan, I'd like for you to meet a friend of mine. This is Joel Edwards." Mr. Hogan looked directly through me and never left eye contact with me, and he stuck out his hand and said, "Joel, it's nice to meet you." And then he says, "I understand you're a rookie this year." And I said, "Yes, sir, I am." And he says, "I tell you what, son, just hang in there. It's going to be tough, but it's also going to be fun. You're going to have some great times, you're going to have some rough times. Don't ever give up. This is what you want to do; do it."

Ben Hogan told me this.

I said, "Yes-ss, ss-sir," and I shook his hand again. He says, "Guys, I'm going to eat lunch and I'd love to sit with you, but I've got a table." He walked over there and sat down, and right as he sat down, he turned around, looked back at me, and said, "Joel, thanks for playing my clubs."

I just looked at him, and he smiled as he sat down. I looked at Mike and he shrugged and said, "I didn't tell him anything." I was carrying a Titleist bag, but I had always played Hogan clubs from the time I was a kid. I birdied nine and eighteen that day at Shady Oaks because I knew he would be watching. I was hoping he would say something more to me, but I never spoke to him again.

At the Kemper Open the next week, I walked up to the Hogan equipment rep and told him this story. He looked at me and he said, "Let me show you something. I have a list of players here who play Hogan equipment, and I want you to see whose name is on top." My name was. The rep then says, "He gets this every week. He knows who you are. He knows what you shot. He knows what shafts you've got. He knows everything about you, so don't you ever think twice that he doesn't know who you are." I just said, "I don't believe this. Ben Hogan knows who I am." It absolutely freaked me out. I'm playing something else now, but I have them made for me and they all look like Hogans.

―――

Understanding Ben Hogan and what made him tick starts with knowing that he didn't grow up in the typical all-American family. His father, Chester, was a blue-collar worker who committed suicide when Ben was nine years old. It is believed that Ben was in the same room when his father put a gun to his head and pulled the trigger. It had to be an absolutely devastating tragedy for the prepubescent Hogan, who went on to become a self-made man. If Hogan had a surrogate father, it was Marvin Leonard, a Fort Worth department store owner a half-

*generation older than Ben. Leonard took Hogan under his wing
when Ben was a teenager and later offered financial support
when Hogan was struggling to launch his professional golf career
in the 1930s and again in the 1950s, when it looked like
Hogan's golf-equipment company might not survive.* **Marty
Leonard,** *one of Marvin's four daughters and a successful amateur golfer and businessperson in her own right, remembers
Hogan as someone akin to a part-time uncle:*

It's saying too much to say he was part of the family
because he wasn't that. But he and my daddy were best
friends, and I grew up with Ben Hogan. Mother and
Daddy would have Ben and Valerie over, but he was also
gone a lot. I certainly recognized who he was and the role
he played, and of course I was very involved in golf growing up. I started swinging a golf club when I was three.
He was definitely my sports hero.

I kept my own little scrapbook on him, which
doesn't amount to much, but I still have it. And of course
it was wonderful for me to have the opportunity to watch
him because he was obviously a legend and, if not the
best, certainly one of the best. I had that opportunity to
see him up close and personal. I remember coming back
when I was in college at SMU to watch the finals of a
playoff involving Hogan at Colonial on a Monday. I
probably skipped school that day. What was painful at
that point was that he was getting to where he was having such a tough time with his putting.

Mostly I watched him at Colonial. It was soon after I
married that he played in that memorable 1960 U.S.
Open in Denver. Mother and Dad and my husband and
I went up on the train, and we stayed at the same hotel
with the Hogans. We didn't see a whole lot of them but

Ben, Princess, and Royal Hogan, probably in their early thirties. This may be the only existing photo of the three children of Chester and Clara Hogan together. (Photograph provided courtesy of Jacqueline Hogan Towery)

we had dinner with them. That was one of the most heartbreaking times that I remember, with Nicklaus, Palmer, and Hogan all going at it. I followed Hogan every step of the way, and I remember when he hit that shot on Sunday at the seventeenth, where his ball hit on the green and spun back into the water. Everybody was just heartbroken. It was also my first look at Nicklaus. It was a fascinating tournament to watch. But I remember going out into the parking lot to be by myself, and I just cried. I was just so upset that he didn't win.

Even though Marvin Leonard was close to being a father figure to Hogan, their mutual respect for each other and similar business philosophies forged a strong relationship that persevered through the decades, as **Marty Leonard** *continues:*

I guess there was enough difference in their ages that it could have been a father-son kind of thing; that Daddy was the sort of father that Ben never really had. I don't know whether that's true or not. But Ben never verbalized that. There was a lot of mutual respect for each other. They liked each other and enjoyed each other. Now, they didn't always agree. Ben tried to give advice when Daddy was building Shady Oaks. Both were very strong-willed men, and so they had their own opinions.

When a book was being written on my father a few years ago, we went to Ben's office so he could be interviewed for the book, although this was when Ben was not as mentally alert as he had been. I remember calling Valerie and telling her, and she said, "You know, Ben's memory is pretty much gone and he can't remember all these things." And I said, "But maybe you can, and you can help."

We went to his office in the old Western Building, sat down, and explained what we were doing. When they asked questions, Valerie would really jump in because he just didn't have any recollection at that point. Anyway, we got through the conversation and he was very gracious. He could be the most gracious person and a true gentleman. He was a pretty straitlaced kind of person, and I never heard him use any foul language. He always had his hat on, and if a lady came into the room, he would always stand up. You don't see much of that nowadays.

About the only thing he said that day was that my dad did more things for more people than anybody ever knew about. It was just the way he functioned. And he said, "He is the finest man I ever knew." He would say the same thing every time, and probably that's about all he could remember. We finally left, thanked them, and walked down the hall. We got all the way down to the elevator, and Ben came back out the door and said, "Wait, wait, wait. I've got something to tell you." So we stopped, and he said the same thing again. He said Daddy was just the finest man he had ever known. At least it tells you something about their relationship. They became friends long before Ben ever got famous, and Daddy helped him some financially in the earlier years.

One of the other great stories that Hogan told, and I wish I had gotten this on video, was when we dedicated the Leonard Room out at Colonial. He and Valerie came to dinner, and we just pretty much had my immediate family and a few close friends there. It was a small affair. We privately dedicated the room and had dinner in the Hogan Room. He told some stories, and one was—and I heard Valerie tell this later—the time he came back to my father and said, "Okay, Marvin, now I want to pay you back for the money that you gave me." And Daddy said, "Well, Bennie, you can't do that. Ben, all I ever cared, all I ever wanted to hear, was for you to say that you intend to pay me back. You can't pay me back." That was typical of my father. And Ben teared up when he told the story. Valerie vaguely remembered some time when Daddy was in San Antonio watching Ben in some tournament and that Ben again tried the same thing, and Daddy wouldn't accept it. Later we found a typed sheet of paper in my father's office, dated 1931, I think. It said, "Marvin Leonard loaned Ben Hogan $300," and then it had some dates and said to wire some more money. At the bottom it said, "Ben Hogan came in the office to visit with Marvin Leonard." It was an original—it had to be original because we found it in Daddy's office. We had it framed and put it out on display at Colonial.

I know he loved my father very much, there's no doubt about that. I know that in a lot of different ways he tried to emulate him. He went about it in a quiet sort of way. They wanted to lead private lives, and they did. That was what they chose to do. But they still had their way of doing things for other people.

———

Jacqueline Hogan Towery of Fort Worth is Hogan's niece, the daughter of his older brother Royal Hogan (who predeceased his brother by a year). Ben and Valerie Hogan never had any children, but Jacque Hogan was probably as close to a son or daughter as the Hogans could have had:

Ben and I were a lot alike. His birthday was August 13, and mine is August 18, so we shared a lot of the same character traits. I suspect that I understood him as well as anyone, including Valerie and my dad, Royal. A lot of people think they knew Ben Hogan, but they didn't know him at all. He was very private but a very warm and loving person. His private life was very personal to him, and he didn't share that part of himself very often with very many people. He was very much a homebody who didn't enjoy the public limelight. Going through the ticker-tape parade in New York following his British

Open victory was probably the hardest thing he ever did, although he was very appreciative.

Being the only child in the Hogan family for fifteen years, I was the center of attention. My brother, Royal Dean, was born when I was in high school, but he died a very young man. I was once again the only child, and I spent a lot of time with Uncle Ben. My grandfather, Chester Hogan, died when his children were very young, so the family consisted of Clara (Mama Hogan), Princess (the oldest child), Royal (my father), and Ben (the youngest). They moved from Dublin, Texas, to Fort Worth, where the children were raised.

When I was growing up, Ben was always at our house for Thanksgiving, Christmas, and birthdays. We were a small family and very close. Nearly everyone loved Mama Hogan, Ben and Daddy adored Princess, and the two boys were pretty good buddies. Ben called Daddy "Bubba," and when my father died in 1996, all Ben could say was, "I can't believe Bubba is gone." He had always been there for Ben, even when they were children.

Traveling as much as he did during his successful years, there wasn't much time for the rest of the family. But he and my father always took good care of their mother. This was a family who had gone through some rough times, and they were fortunate just to survive. I know that Mama Hogan was greatly responsible for the success that Ben and Daddy experienced. She believed in doing something right, and if it wasn't right, do it again. She taught me to sew when I was twelve years old, and when I didn't get a stitch the way she taught me, she had me rip it out and start over. As a result, I am a very good seamstress, and I have made my own clothes most of my life.

Christmas always brings back some wonderful memories for me. It became a family joke about presents. My mother and father, Uncle Ben and Valerie, Princess and Uncle Doc, and Mama Hogan all knew what was wrapped before they received the gift. The men got pajamas with initials embroidered on the pocket, and house slippers. The women got a slip or a gown, the same year after year. It was, "Oh, thank you. This is just what I needed," and everyone laughed.

In the summertime Daddy made peach ice cream in the old ice cream freezer. He would pour in the ice and the rock salt, and I would sit on the top while he turned the handle. Peach was Ben's favorite flavor of ice cream, and he would eat a lot of it. Once, when he had eaten about five bowls full, he said, "Bubba, there's salt in this ice cream." We all had a good laugh because Ben finally could not eat any more. Every time we had peach ice cream, Daddy reminded Uncle Ben about the salt.

—————

Hogan played his last competitive round of golf in the early 1970s and then retired to a life of relative seclusion. To find him, one would best pay a morning visit to the Hogan Company or head out to Shady Oaks, where Hogan would take up residence at a large roundtable in a corner of the men's grill. The greens of both the ninth and eighteenth holes were clearly visible from Hogan's seat. Shady Oaks head pro **Mike Wright** *could set his watch every weekday by Hogan's imminent arrival:*

His routine was that he would get to the club about 11:30 and have lunch with his friends. Every day we would anticipate that he was going to go out and hit golf balls.

Valerie and Ben Hogan and their niece Jacque Hogan Towery, circa 1992.
(Photograph provided courtesy of Jacqueline Hogan Towery)

So we kept his bag in the bag room. By 12:30 or 1:00 somebody would check to see if Mr. Hogan was planning on hitting balls. We would put his clubs right outside the golf shop door, and we kept his shag balls under the counter so nobody would mess with them. And we would put his clubs on a rack—it was a very conservative bag, a maroon bag, not a red-white-and-blue Hogan bag or anything like that. We would then slant it on the cart sideways so that the clubs would be easy to get to from the driver's side. Also, we would wrap a half-wet towel to the cart and put his shag balls in the seat so that when he went out he could immediately see everything was the way he wanted it.

—⟨⟩—

Occupying a seat at Hogan's lunchtime table wasn't as easy as taking a number and waiting your turn. Invitations were harder to get than a tee time at Augusta National. Fort Worth geologist **Bob Wynne** *and* **Gene Smyers** *made the short list and stayed there for many years:*

Wynne: In 1971 I joined Shady Oaks and, of course, saw Mr. Hogan all the time and knew who he was. He always returned hellos and was very cordial, but you didn't just join him at his table and become a friend. One day a friend of mine asked me to join him for lunch at the table to discuss a geological situation. Hogan never entered the conversation, but several days later he asked me to join him for conversation. That's how our friendship started and we became rather close friends.

Smyers: We'd come out here and Charles (head waiter Charles Hudson) would wait on us day after day, and nobody would sit in the chair where Mr. (Earl) Baldridge had sat before he passed away. And since Ben died, none of us have been back to that table for lunch. I think I've eaten there once: I had my whole family out one night for a birthday and it was the only available table, so we sat there.

He would sit here and observe golfers. On occasion he would make some comment about someone who had a good golf swing. Ben was very observant. He was an intense student of a lot of things. For someone who didn't have a lot of education, Ben was very intelligent. When they honored Marty's father at Colonial, Ben spoke, and he was very articulate. His remarks were very pertinent; they were well chosen and well spoken.

---

*Kris Tschetter, an LPGA tour veteran who played her college golf at Texas Christian University in Fort Worth, and who joined Shady Oaks with her family in the early eighties, never took up permanent residence at the Hogan roundtable. But she became one of the handful of professional golfers able to benefit from Hogan's longtime tutelage. **Bob Wynne** helped lay the groundwork for Tschetter to meet Hogan, as he explains here, followed by Tschetter's take on how she finally got around to meeting him:*

Wynne: I was golf chairman at Shady Oaks for six years. Kris Tschetter was on the TCU women's golf team, and she became close friends with my wife and me. She obviously wanted to know Hogan, and I knew how to make it happen. I would tell him how she had a grandfather who had built a bunker in their basement in South Dakota, or how nice her folks were and how well she was doing on TCU's golf team. He never said anything, but I knew he was formulating in her mind that she was okay. Kris has a nice personality and is a good golfer. She also practiced where Hogan had practiced and where he walked in the afternoons, so their friendship evolved over a period of time.

Tschetter: I was never really introduced to him. When my brother (Mike) and I first became members of Shady Oaks, part of the unwritten rule out there was that Mr. Hogan is just left alone. He really liked his privacy and he didn't want anyone making a big deal out of him. Basically, we were told, "If Mr. Hogan talks to you, that's fine, but you don't ever say anything to him." When I would see him, I would act like I didn't see him. And then I thought, "I'm not going to treat him any differently than all the other men out here that I say hello to when they walk by." So I just started saying hello to him. The first real conversation I remember having with him other than "Hi, Mr. Hogan" was when I was hitting some balls one time on the little nine at Shady Oaks. He stopped and gave me a little tip, watched me hit a few, and then walked off.

That would happen quite often. I would be out on the little nine or whatever and he would walk by, say hello, and stop and look. He'd maybe say something and then walk on. One day he comes up and says, "This is what you've got to do," and he started to show me something. I said, "Well, Mr. Hogan, maybe I'd get a better idea if I saw you do it." So he dropped these three balls.

I think he had a six- or seven-iron, and he hit three of the prettiest shots right onto the green.

He said, "How's that?"

I said, "It looked pretty good, and now I understand it." Then he walked off. That was the first time that I ever got up the nerve to ask for more than what he was offering. When we first started working together, he would have only one club and go out with his three balls, and he would walk around the little nine at Shady Oaks. Then it got to a point where he would get his shag bag and his clubs, and come out to the little nine to practice. Eventually, he would come to wherever I was hitting, or I'd go to wherever he was hitting—depending on who got there first. He would hit his shag bag, I'd hit mine, and then we'd go pick them up. When he got tired, he would just watch me hit and then he would help me pick them up. I always say that I'm the only person who ever had Hogan shagging for him or her.

I spent as much time with him as I could. I was so lucky just to be able to see him hit as many balls as I did. I know so little about the golf swing that I don't think I picked up as much about the golf swing from him as someone else with more knowledge would have. Even to this day I'll say things to my husband, Kirk Lucas, who is my teacher, "Mr. Hogan always used to say this to me," and Kirk will say, "Oh, I think what he was trying to say or trying to get you to do was . . ." Mr. Hogan was such a feel player. What he felt and what he did were really two different things. He probably had a lot of knowledge of the golf swing, but it was hard communicating it to me.

A lot of times when he was out at Shady Oaks, he would give someone a tip and they would get it

21

overdone. It would end up hurting them more than helping them. He spent a lot of time with me to where he was able to help me quite a bit, although I think I learned more about managing my game than actual swing stuff. More than anything, I learned from him how to hit certain shots at certain times. When the shot called for a fade, you hit a fade. When it called for a draw, you hit a draw. You learned to hit all of the shots so you have them when you need them. And I have a lot of the shots. I may not pull them all off, but at least I've got them. I guess you could say that I'm more of a shotmaker than a lot of the other women on the (LPGA) tour.

—⸱⸱⸱—

*When she wasn't out playing tour events, **Tschetter** called Fort Worth home for a number of years. Returning to her home base gave her a chance to hit shag balls with Hogan at Shady Oaks, although she occasionally got to know more about the man during off-course time with the legendary golfer and his wife, Valerie:*

My husband (Kirk Lucas) and I had dinner one time with them, which was a thrill for Kirk because he's just a golf student. He's a great teacher and is always trying to gain knowledge whenever he can. He asked so many questions that Mr. Hogan kept leaning over and going, "Is this guy a reporter?" And I'd say, "No, no; now, c'mon."

Another thing people didn't realize about him was how sensitive he was—how much he loved Valerie and how he so appreciated what she sacrificed for him. People kind of think of him as this cold-hearted person, but he so wasn't that. He was this wonderfully sensitive man with a great sense of humor. I met him at a time when I'm sure he had softened quite a bit, so my perception of him is very different. No matter what, though, I'm sure that side was always there and he just didn't expose it to a lot of people.

———

Veteran PGA Tour golfer **Tom Byrum** *got to know Hogan in part through his friendship with Kris Tschetter. Byrum said he and Tschetter dated back in the 1980s (they're both from South Dakota), and it was through Tschetter's existing friendship with Hogan at Shady Oaks Country Club that the low-key Byrum— who could pass for a young Hogan's stunt double from a distance, both with the golf swing and the physique—got to know the man. Through his relationship with Tschetter, Byrum got to know not only Hogan, but also many of his Shady Oaks cronies as well, including geologist Bob Wynne, who, along with seventeen other people, formed a group to help sponsor Byrum during his early years on the PGA Tour. Byrum explains:*

After qualifying for the tour and meeting Mr. Hogan, Bob Wynne and I were out at Shady one day to have lunch. We sat with Hogan. He asked me what kind of clubs I played. They were not Hogan. He set me up to go down to the factory the next day and get set up with some Hogan clubs. So Bob Wynne got me "in" with him after Kris had introduced us. Hogan really liked Kris, who was in college at the time. Really, all the members liked her and her brother Mike around the club.

    Having the eighteen guys following me on tour made it easy for me to fit in at Shady. They were very good to me out there, and because of my being around there a lot, I think Hogan gained an interest in me. We had two things in common: We were both tour players and we both used Hogan irons. That was a big thing to him. I think he also grew to trust me because I wouldn't tell anyone what he and I would talk about. He had told me not to. Same thing when he showed me something about the golf swing; I didn't pass it on because he told me he didn't want to read it in some magazine.

I think people had, and have, the wrong impression of the man because of his accomplishments. All they saw was "the Hawk" or "the Ice Man," which is what he was when he was trying to win. I saw a very private man almost too shy to meet people. And he didn't have all the "secrets" people thought he had. He had found what worked for him, and he was reluctant to tell people what it was because he knew it wouldn't work for them.

<hr />

Fort Worth physician **Dr. Jim Murphy** *was a Hogan round-table regular, who knew Hogan well for another reason: He was the Hawk's personal physician for the last thirty-five years of Hogan's life:*

For probably twenty-five years, I was a member at Shady Oaks and I used to play golf on Wednesdays over there. I always had lunch at the big table, and Ben was always there. It was just the usual kind of conversation you have when you sit at a roundtable with about eight or ten guys. Ben wasn't the kind of guy that you just sat around and shot the (breeze) with. First of all, I was busy as hell, and he was busy, and we just never had any really intimate conversations. It was mostly a pretty businesslike deal.

---

*Also, as **Dr. Murphy** points out, there were no "longhairs" welcomed at Hogan's table:*

He could not tolerate a hippie-style person at all. If you didn't have a good, short haircut, he was ticked. He was quite a character, and if you brushed him the wrong way, he could be awfully brusque.

---

*As much as Hogan didn't like long hair, try finding a photo of him with a buzz cut. It probably doesn't exist. Senior PGA Tour veteran **Jim Ferree,** whose early pro career overlapped with Hogan's twilight years, talk's about Hogan's penchant for style:*

Hogan always looked like he needed a haircut. He had long hair when most people didn't have long hair. But he got a lot of haircuts, maybe every week or two weeks, but that barber—Colonial had its own barber—did not cut much hair off. When most people cut their hair, they try to keep in mind what it will look like in a week to ten days. But Ben would ask to have it cut in such a way that it would not look like he had had a haircut, period.

His hair was longer, but it was nice-looking. He managed everything very closely: his clubs, the balls he played, the clothes he wore. Once he got pretty successful, he could afford really nice clothes, and he would never get pants with a zipper. He always wanted pants with buttons in front because it was just one more little precaution for when he was playing. If he needed to go to the restroom and the zipper wouldn't go down, then it would be very difficult to go. Or if you got it down and then it wouldn't go back up, he would have to go back out and play with his fly open. Also, he wore very nice-looking slacks. You can tell just by looking at any of the pictures from the years he played. I look at (Byron) Nelson, (Sam) Snead, and those boys of that era, and, although they didn't have near the money that the boys of today have, I thought they dressed much more gentle-manly or elegantly or whatever you want to call it. These days we've got guys making millions of dollars and they're out there in painter's pants and that kind of stuff that you can just walk into any ol' department store and buy. But I love to look at those old pictures of Ben and Byron and Sam and Vic Ghezzi—like when they were at an awards presentation. They were never without a sport coat.

One thing Hogan apparently didn't like was heights, as his niece **Jacqueline Hogan Towery** *explains:*

Once when Ben checked into a hotel in Chicago, they gave him a room on the twenty-first floor. He rode the elevator up to the twenty-first floor, went into the room, looked out the window, and got his bags and went back to the lobby. At the desk he asked them to find him another room on a lower floor. They didn't have one, so he moved to another hotel. When the Petroleum Club in Fort Worth moved to the top floor, the thirty-second floor, he canceled his membership. He hated high places, and he didn't care much for airplanes. I truly believe that this was the main reason he played only once in the British Open.

———⚜———

Golf, obviously, was Hogan's best game. Gin rummy wasn't. Although Hogan was an avid card player for many years, long time family friend **W. A. "Tex" Moncrief** *is all the richer for having sat across the card table from Hogan:*

I saw him just about every day that he was at Shady Oaks Country Club. I used to play a lot of golf there, and we also had a gin rummy game at Shady Oaks. I'd be there most every afternoon after I got through working downtown, usually around four o'clock. And, of course, Ben sat there at one particular spot at the table. In fact, we've got a marker on it now. He'd be there every day at lunch. He would go to his Hogan Golf Company in the morning and then he would get out there about 11:45 or 12:00 and have a glass of wine or a martini. Of course he used to practice a lot several years before his death, but then as he began to get a little bit weaker and all that, he quit practicing.

But even after he quit, I would see him every damn day. And he would be sitting there and sometimes he would come over and stand and watch us play gin. He used to play gin with us, but he was the slowest player in the world and one of the sorriest gin players I ever met. Oh, hell, he couldn't play gin at all. And he started playing gin, I guess, back over at Rivercrest Country Club.

Our normal game back then was fifty cents a point and fifty bucks a hand. And we got into the game with Marvin and Ben. A lot of times during the day, if he got behind or something, we would double up and start playing a dollar a point and a hundred dollars a hand. And they played us about four or five days, and we took several thousand dollars off them. And Ben quit.

—⚬—

Betting on football didn't seem to offer much of a reprieve, either, as **Moncrief** *adds:*

He always liked to bet on football, too. He and Earl Baldridge would be out there Friday or Saturday morning before the games start, and Ben would come up with what they called a Blue Plate Special. And if he even got half of them right, I think he would have been lucky. But he would just sit there and bet with them, and a lot of times I would take just the opposite of what Ben was doing, and I won money off of him. And he eventually quit betting on football.

—⚬—

What did Hogan like to eat at Shady Oaks? A little bit brunch and a touch of soup, as head waiter **Charles Hudson**—*who has been at Shady Oaks since it opened in 1958—points out:*

I waited on him almost every day. He would order a cup of bean soup, toast, bacon, stuff like that. He would eat a junior club. He would eat scrambled eggs and bacon.

—⚬—

*When it came to eating a meal, Hogan was as precise in his
choice of condiments as he was in picking clubs for his shots on
the golf course, as his niece **Jacqueline Hogan Towery** can
testify:*

Around the time I was about twelve years old and into
my teenage years, my father, mother, and I for several
years spent summers following the tour. We would go
from one tournament to the next, and, believe it or not,
it was a fun way to spend my summer vacation. We
didn't spend much time with Ben during the tournament, because when he wasn't playing a tournament
round he was playing a practice round and hitting practice balls early and late. Sometimes we traveled in separate cars, but when we traveled by train we were together.
One time in the dining car Ben ordered a steak, and
when the waiter brought it to the table, Ben asked for
A-1 Sauce. The waiter told him what a good piece of
meat it was and that it didn't need any sauce. Ben said,
"It's my steak, and I want A-1 Sauce!" He got the sauce
and used it.

———

*Hogan was a golf traditionalist right down to the clubhouse
rules, starting with "no women in the men's locker room," even
when that woman happened to be **Marty Leonard,** an officer
of the club in there on official business:*

In his later years, back when my dad was gone and I happened to be chairman of the house committee here at
Shady Oaks, we were talking about redoing some things
in the men's locker room. One morning I went in there

to look at it, and of course I don't go in the men's locker room very often. I was in there looking around and we were trying to decide on a decorator, and we were trying to decide how to redo this or redo that. And Ben walks in through the door. I'll never forget this: He walked in, stopped, and looked at me. I don't remember exactly what he said. But whatever it was, he didn't think I had any business being in there; I know that for sure. I said something and he turned around and walked back out. He later came back in, but I didn't stay in there very long.

Shady Oaks head pro **Mike Wright** *not only talked shop with Hogan on numerous occasions, he also found himself playing bodyguard—shielding Hogan from the occasional curiosity seekers whose sole purpose for being at Shady Oaks was to catch a glimpse of "da man":*

A guy in my shoes should have probably kept track of every little experience I had with him, but that probably would have been cheating. You don't do that to friends. I just remember that near the end, I tried to be careful not to put him into a situation that he might be uncomfortable with that day. Even on a questionable day, he was always incredibly hospitable to guests. He was extremely friendly and genuine, and he cared and had interest in people and that kind of thing.

One February day we were standing in the golf shop. I remember that it was real cold, and some people from Florida came to the club. Mr. Hogan and I had been talking for about an hour. I remember thinking, "I hope nobody comes in today," and sure enough here comes these three guys from Florida. They walk into Shady Oaks, and the only reason they were here was to see where Ben Hogan hangs out. And there's Ben Hogan, the first person they see, and me. They were stunned, and, of course, they asked a couple of questions, very stock-type stuff. He answered and, trying not to be rude, he elaborated a little bit but not very much. I could tell that he was uncomfortable, and yet he and I had been standing there talking for about an hour. They stayed maybe ten minutes and then left, although he usually would be the one to leave first. Then he turned around and said, "That's the hard part, Mike, 'cause these gentlemen will repeat what I said and that story will be changed several times, and that makes me uncomfortable."

Byron Nelson knew Ben Hogan for more than seventy years. They were peers as fellow Fort Worth–area natives, pro-golf rivals for more than twenty years and lifelong Dallas–Fort Worth residents. They and their wives even traveled together during their early years playing the tour. Did they respect each other? Undoubtedly. Did they speak to one another and keep in touch? Some. But were they chummy? Not exactly. If Nelson had ever wanted to get to know Hogan better than he did, he knew it would have been a tough nut to crack:

Ben has never liked being around a lot of people and that's fine. It's his business and I respect that. But I always thought it was a shame in a way because he missed so much. People idolized him so, and to a certain extent that can be a very good thing. I know the way people feel about me has always made me feel good and made me want to try hard to be a better person. It's difficult for people to get a chance to interview Ben, so they ask me about him a lot, but I just don't particularly like to talk about him. I feel like that's invading his privacy, so I don't say much. We've always gotten along fine and we've always liked each other very much. We're simply different personalities, and there's nothing wrong with that.[1]

As long as **Nelson** *knew Hogan, he came to know that he never really knew him, as he mentioned to this author in a 1989 Fort Worth Star-Telegram interview:*

I've known him since I was twelve years old, and it's hard to understand how he feels. I really don't know enough about Ben to know what makes him tick. I heard him say one time that people were complaining about the fact that he doesn't talk enough or isn't friendly enough on the course, when [he says], "I'm just trying to play golf in the best form."

Gene Smyers *witnessed a hint of sincere warmth in the Hogan-Nelson relationship at the funeral of Nelson's first wife, Louise, in the mid-1980s:*

I saw Ben and Valerie go to Byron and both of them put their arms around him, and he gave them a big hug and it was sincerity and it was genuine. Of course, both of them were very sincere. There was an affection and admiration and respect. I know, Ben wasn't as cordial to Byron as I would have hoped he would have been, because Byron was such a gentleman. Yet there was a great deal of respect and I had an opportunity to be with Byron many, many times in the last twenty years, especially down at Kerrville. And on that occasion, it was evident. And Byron, of course, was at Ben's funeral and he was at Valerie's funeral.

———

Jerry Austry still lives and works in Fort Worth, although it has been more than ten years since he was jettisoned from his position as president of the Hogan Company after it was sold in late 1988. Austry worked for the Hogan Company for about five years, and his almost-daily contact with Hogan gave him ample opportunities to see Hogan's persona up close:

Ben had two personalities. He was very kind for the most part, but if he perceived that someone was encroaching on him, he could really rip them. I was petrified working for him. People would hide from him. He would get up in sales meetings and rip my predecessor as president, Roger Corbett, and I think the reason for that was because he was kept in the dark. Attempts had been made to insulate him from the decision-making process in and around the company. At other times, though, he would show up at sales meetings attended by the pros playing our clubs and he couldn't have been nicer. That's when he turned on the charm.

———

John Mahaffey, a relative newcomer to the Senior PGA Tour, and the 1978 PGA Championship winner, first met Hogan around 1970, when he was playing collegiate golf for the University of Houston. Their good friendship was almost instantaneous, which is somewhat surprising from the standpoint that Mahaffey is a relatively outgoing person with a quick trigger on the humor front:

Most people misunderstood Ben Hogan. I think he really wanted to be more personable, but he was very shy. I heard him speak on a number of occasions, and he had a wonderful message, but it was almost like he was embarrassed to get up there and say anything. I don't know why, but a lot of people are like that.

He was always very good to me and I'll never forget him. His demeanor on the golf course might not have been what people would have liked, but it fit his personality very much as a professional's professional. He liked people who were fighters. I played pretty much like him. I will never say that I had Hogan's swing—I wish I did—but it was pretty similar in a lot of ways. I think he saw some potential there, and I think he enjoyed playing with me. We had some camaraderie.

I'm pretty proud of the fact that by the time I went on to the PGA Tour I had worked for Jimmy Demaret and Jackie Burke at Champions and had made friends with Ben Hogan. I had to fill out an application to go to tour school and had to have three people sign it, and my three were Jackie Burke, Ben Hogan, and Jimmy Demaret. That's something that I will never forget.

John Jacobs, also a Senior PGA Tour, was on the Hogan Company staff as a player rep playing Hogan clubs for two years:

I think Hogan had a side that he didn't have any room for small talk such as shootin' the breeze or talking about other sporting events. When you were with him on the golf course, there was no time for small talk. But he was gracious to me. I had dinner with him twice. I was at his testimonial dinner—there were probably twenty-five pros there—when he broke down and cried because he was losing his company to AMF (in 1993). It was pitiful to see him break down in tears.

———

Longtime Fort Worth Star-Telegram *sportswriter and columnist* **Galyn Wilkins** *remembers being assigned to cover one of Hogan's rare tournament appearances after 1960, that being the Carling World Open played at Oakland Hills outside Detroit. Wilkins had never met Hogan, but he had heard of his reputation, and went to Detroit with trepidation:*

I knew that the Hogan Company was wanting to make a big splash at the time. After I got up there, I went to the locker room, having never been face to face with Hogan. To say I was intimidated was an understatement. I had heard stories of his being cold and nontalkative. When I approached him, he asked me to sit down. He was sitting there with one shoe on and one shoe off. We talked for what must have been forty-five minutes, and he told me that he never had gotten the thrill to compete out of his system. I thought that maybe he was just being accommodating to me because he was trying to sell his line of golf clubs, but after a while I felt he was being sincere in saying he had the urge to come back.

On another occasion, also in the sixties, I went to Wichita Falls (Texas) to cover a junior golf association banquet at which Hogan was the keynote speaker. It turned out to be a really nice event, and he made a really nice speech about how to compete with honor, as gentlemen, and that he had never gotten over the love of competition. I was really impressed.

(In a testimonial *Star-Telegram* story written after Hogan's death, Wilkins expanded on the banquet-speech story:) He looked at the kids, not at a page of notes. It was something they probably had heard from the pulpit the previous Sunday, but this time they were listening. A last impression from that evening was Hogan's diction. I was surprised then, and in future conversations, that he didn't talk like other Texans, certainly not one whose vocabulary was enriched in the Glen Garden caddie shack. He spoke like he swung a five-iron, with a direct, economical purity and without the barest hint of a Fort Worth twang.

---

*CBS-TV golf analyst **Ken Venturi,** the 1964 U.S. Open champion, probably was as close to Hogan as any other professional golfer. They met at the 1954 Masters, when Venturi was still a highly touted amateur. Almost thirty years later, they got together for one of the most memorable interviews in televised-sports history. Venturi's voice still cracks when he recalls that spring day in 1983:*

(CBS golf executive producer) Frank Chirkinian asked Ben Hogan if he would do the interview. We went out to Shady Oaks to ask him. He said yes, and it was the first one that he had granted (to CBS). He said, however, "I will do it only if nobody's around, and the only one who can interview me is Ken Venturi. That's the only one I want to have." And so we sat there, and I had a bunch of questions I had written out. We sat side by side facing each other, and he was just an arm's length away from me. I asked the first question, and I never looked down at my notes again because he never took his eyes off me. He was talking right to me, and I had to start thinking while he was talking what the hell my next question was. This was continuous. There was no break.

When we got going, the things that we spoke of included the time in Oakland (in 1938) when he had his tires stolen off his car and he won that ($385) check, and he's always said it was still the biggest check he ever saw in his life. He got teary-eyed—kind of choked up and the whole thing—and we just riveted right on each other. His eyes were right on mine. He was very comfortable with all my questions because I never threw him any curves. He trusted me so well that the things I asked him were the things that he could answer and nothing that he would hedge on. After the interview, we went in and had lunch at Shady Oaks. I guess he knew and trusted our friendship because of the tremendous respect I had for him.

After Hogan passed away in July 1997, Valerie Hogan called **Venturi** *and asked him to be one of the pallbearers. This was not long after Venturi's wife, Beau, had passed away:*

Ben died just a short time after my wife, Beau, died. Valerie called me to tell me that Ben had just passed away. And I was just so taken aback just as I would be if I were to hear that Byron had passed away—it would be the same thing. My admiration for both of them is just, it's just untold. So she asked; she said that Ben had passed away. I believe I was at Hartford, and it was just a short time after Beau had passed away. I said, "I'll be there." But she said, "Oh, no, no, Ken, with what you're going through, you don't have to. I just wanted you to know that Ben had passed away and he had wanted you to know first." So I was one of the very, very first calls that were made, and she found me. So I flew down to Fort Worth and they had me picked up and dropped me off at a hotel. After I got there, she said, "Would you be a pallbearer? You were Ben's first choice." And I said, "Valerie, I would be honored."

A handful of golfers who shared at least some time on the same golf stage with Hogan were said to be his friends, but even that might have been a stretch. Hogan peer Jimmy Demaret wrote a book about Hogan, but little of what Demaret wrote broke any new ground in revealing "the real Ben Hogan." Sam Snead was a close rival for many years, but their paths rarely crossed away from the golf course. Byron Nelson knew Hogan from the time they were both twelve, but they have for the most part operated in different worlds despite living only thirty miles apart. Among the professional golfers who hobnobbed with Hogan away from the glare of competitive golf were Gardner Dickinson, and brothers Jay and Lionel Hebert. Although about twenty years younger than Hogan, Lionel Hebert enjoyed close access to Hogan over the years, which meant putting up with a fair amount of teasing from Hogan. Still, to be teased by Hogan was a form of special affection. **Lionel Hebert,** *the 1957 PGA champion, remembers:*

I had read a lot about Hogan before I met him, and I got to know him through my affiliation with Gardner Dickinson, who had been a friend of mine while we were going to LSU. Gardner, my brother Jay, and I were all good friends. After Gardner first turned pro, he went to Palm Springs to work for Hogan. I like Hogan. He was a helluva guy. He liked to tease me a lot. I ended up playing a lot of practice rounds with him over the years. In tournaments, after I finished my round, I would go back out to watch him play if he was still out on the golf course. He was a great striker of the golf ball. He loved to control the ball and one thing was that he would never lose the ball in the wind. He always knew how to allow for things such as the wind.

If he could have putted at all when he got older, there's no telling what else he could have done in his career. Maybe he used up all his good putts at an earlier age. I used to see him play a lot at Colonial. One time I remember in particular was when I played thirty-six holes with him and shot two rounds of 67, which was a record at the time for Colonial. After we finished out at eighteen, he called a photographer over and said, "You've got to see this young man," and he had a photo of us taken right there.

————

Follow the Sun, *a 1951 movie on Hogan's life up to and including his 1949 automobile accident and his subsequent recovery, will never make top-ten lists when it comes to rating the best sports movies of all time. Glenn Ford and Academy Award–winning actress Anne Baxter played Ben and Valerie in a film filled with clichés, sappy sentimentality, and awkward close-up golf-swing scenes with the nongolfing Ford. But it remains a fascinating piece of pop culture, and it certainly had an impact on Hogan, who, joined by* **Bob Wynne,** *watched a video of the movie about forty years after its release. Wynne recalls:*

One day he left the Nineteenth Hole and came back with the videotape *Follow the Sun*. He had Charles Hudson, the Nineteenth Hole manager, set everything up for viewing, and we watched it together. It was a very emotional experience for him. I don't know how long it had been since he had last seen it, but we sat there and watched it for a while. Pretty well into it, he turned to me and said, "Bob, I don't even remember that." Then he got to a part in it that he did remember, and he just teared up. He didn't sob or cry, but then he just got up and left. I don't remember what part of the movie it was.

————

Wynne *further remembers that Hogan had other soft spots, especially when it came to dogs and children:*

Everyone's heard about the dogs, Max and Buster, that hung around at Shady Oaks—not at the same time. Max was the first one, but he got run over by a delivery truck. Then we had Buster. Hogan was the reason they were there (at different times). He would cut up a steak and put it out there for them. He loved children and dogs. If a child would walk by, he would just brighten up. He never did that with an adult person.

Ben loved dogs, including a poodle named Duffer he once owned. **Doxie Williams,** *for thirteen years Hogan's administrative assistant at the Hogan Company, remembers just how much Duffer meant to Hogan and how some of Hogan's friends tried to comfort him in a time of sorrow:*

He was so soft hearted, and I even saw him shed tears on several occasions. For many years he had a poodle named Duffer and he simply adored that dog, which died in his arms. This is hearsay, but I understand that he said he never wanted to have another dog after losing Duffer. Still, some friends of his from the East Coast wanted to give him another dog for Christmas, and they even had it flown in and driven from the airport over to the Hogans' house. But Ben and Valerie finally decided that they just couldn't take care of it. Their yard wasn't fenced in and if it were icy or cold outside, they wouldn't be able to take the dog out. So they sent the dog back to their friends. The next day Mr. Hogan was telling me about this and he was crying, because the people who had sent them the dog were such good friends of his and Valerie's.

He was always thinking of other people and there were many times that he did things for people he didn't know and which only a few people ever knew about. I remember one time he read about a woman in Wichita Falls (Texas) who had been in an auto accident and had suffered some sort of serious injury to her legs, and he sent a check to her. He would also read about children with terminal illnesses making a wish through something like the Make a Wish Foundation, and he would send out a check. He was such a generous man.

Jacqueline Hogan Towery also remembers "Duffer," Hogan's canine companion, and adds to the story:

There was a period of time when I was in college, then getting married and having four children, when I didn't get to spend much time with Uncle Ben. But I always saw him on holidays, and I took my children to his house on Halloween. Ben loved children. I think he was really sorry that he never had a child. He always treated me like a daughter, and that made a certain (unspecified) person very jealous. The closest thing to a child of his own was a poodle given to him by a Mr. Coleman, probably the best friend Ben ever had. Ben did not want a dog, but in deference to his friend he took him and named him "Duffer." That dog became very special to Uncle Ben and was never left alone. He had a personal sitter when they went anywhere, even to dinner.

Duffer is buried in the back yard of Ben's home, and there was a marker at his grave at one time. Uncle Ben

Ben Hogan in the late 1950s with Duffer, his beloved poodle; Royal Dean Hogan, Ben's nephew; and Clara "Mama" Hogan. (Photograph provided courtesy of Jacqueline Hogan Towery)

befriended another dog at Shady Oaks Country Club. This was just an old dog that hung around, and Uncle Ben would feed him leftovers, or he would order him something. The dog was treated pretty much like a member and had the run of the club.

⋯⋯⋯

Gene Smyers *saw another side of Hogan's generosity, which also was extended to people he did know:*

Ben was a generous man in different ways. We had a waitress that got shot. Rosa Linda. I was here and he tapped me as I walked by him and he said, "Give me two hundred dollars." He gauged what he wanted by who it was. He got five hundred dollars from Tex (Moncrief), Tex's dad, and Eddie Chiles. But, from a lot of them he got a hundred dollars; from others he got two hundred dollars. All told, he got about sixty-eight hundred. And Ben wrote a kid over in Weatherford who had lost his arm in an accident and was just thirteen years old or thereabouts. Ben was touched by him and wrote him a letter of encouragement. Things like this people didn't know. Ben certainly shied away from anything that would bring attention to him.

—————

As much time as Hogan spent dining and socializing with his cronies at Shady Oaks, he would occasionally be joined there by family, which usually meant his brother, Royal, and his niece **Jacqueline Hogan Towery.** *Towery remembers those times fondly:*

In the late 1980s, after all my children were grown, I again had the opportunity to spend a lot of time with Ben, having dinner with him three or four times a week. Occasionally we had dinner in his home, and it was very formal, with servants and more silver than anyone knew how to use. This was not my Uncle Ben; it was Valerie and her house and her rules. Ben liked to go to places he knew and in which he was comfortable, and therefore, we ate at Shady Oaks Country Club most of the time. We always sat at "Mr. Hogan's table." He always sat in the same chair, and he always wanted me to sit to his right.

When we had dinner at Shady Oaks and the weather was bad, we parked upstairs and walked down a curved staircase to the dining room. The first time we did this, as he reached the bottom, he said, "Always the same." I asked him what he said, and he told me, "Always the same number of steps." He counted the steps each time because he wanted to make sure they had not lost one. He had a marvelous sense of humor and the most wonderful, childlike way of clapping his hands when something pleased him. He would hold his hands in a prayer-like position and clap them softly together.

At first my father joined us for dinner, or rather, my father and I joined Ben for dinner. My father didn't care much for Valerie, but he enjoyed Ben's company. Ben and Daddy would argue over who was going to pay the bill. Each would try to trick the other out of the bill, or maybe just pull it out of the other's hand. Those are some of my most cherished memories, seeing them together and hearing them talk about the past and laugh. I loved my father very much, although we clashed a lot. But I adored my Uncle Ben, and he loved me as much as an uncle could love a niece. When we were at dinner he would reach over, hold and pat my hand, and tell me how much he loved me. We really had a great relationship.

———

*At one time **Marty Leonard,** Marvin Leonard's daughter, was one of the top female amateur golfers in north Texas, although Hogan deserves little of the credit. As well and as long as Marty Leonard knew Hogan, little of his golfing prowess rubbed off on Leonard. But where golf was not a common topic of conversation between them, Leonard got to know Ben and Valerie in other off-course settings:*

I never had any golf instruction from him. I watched him

hit some balls from time to time, and I was a fairly decent amateur player at that point. But I didn't go out and play with him a lot. I'm sure we talked about golf some. We talked about anything anybody would normally talk about. I guess I remember eating out here with them several times in later years because they would come out here and eat very regularly until he was no longer well. Even though they had a cook at home, they would still come out and eat a lot. Sometimes I would just come and sit and visit with him. I'm sure we must have talked about my father some. And we probably talked about Shady Oaks some. Their life obviously revolved around golf and him and his career. I'm not going to say their life was narrow because that's not the right word, but it was certainly focused.

—————

Ben and Valerie never had children. What they did have was Ben's nearly obsessive one-track life, which for many years was primarily golf competition. Valerie's total commitment was to Ben and taking care of her man, which helps explain the following observation from **Marty Leonard:**

I remember Valerie saying the day they opened Ben's room at the USGA Golf House that "You know God's in heaven and all's right with the world" kind of comment. Her death was almost like one of those where she just sort of felt that she had accomplished what she had set out to accomplish, and that was to see his trophy collection at the Golf House through. I was amazed that she was there because she was pretty fragile. She had pneumonia and was never quite the same after that. She was a strong woman constitution-wise, but physically she was small. You just didn't think of her as being terribly strong and she had been through all his illnesses. She developed some problems that were probably just stress related. I'm sure they never even got diagnosed really. I don't know whether it was the shingles or whatever, but she had some problems.

It was apparently Valerie's decision to have Hogan's golf memorabilia collection moved from Colonial Country Club to the USGA Museum in New Jersey following Hogan's death in 1997. **Jacqueline Hogan Towery,** *the Hogans' niece, paints the picture:*

Uncle Ben's favorite color was red, as is mine, but there was not one thing red in his home. It was very formal and had Valerie's blue and white throughout, except for one bathroom that was yellow. There were no trophies or golf items on shelves or mantels and no pictures of Ben relating to golf. Golf was Ben's life, his profession, his hobby, and his everyday activity. He loved golf, and he was thankful for what golf had done for him. I think he fully realized the responsibility he had to the sport he mastered. I do not believe that he ever wanted his memorabilia to be moved away from Fort Worth and the Colonial, which had been so instrumental in his career.

Just before Ben's death, Valerie did not want me to come to see him. She tried to keep it from me that he was taken to the hospital, but a friend called me, and I rushed over. I was his closest blood relative after Daddy died, and I had called numerous times to ask about him and ask to come see him. Knowing that he had Alzheimer's disease, I had offered to come over and sit with him and give Valerie a break. However, I was denied the right to see him for over two years prior to his death. Respecting Uncle Ben's desire for privacy, I didn't force the issue. I wish now that I had, and this time no one could keep me from seeing him. Valerie looked shocked to see me there, but she couldn't stop me. I went into his room, patted his hand, and told him that it was Jacqueline (he pronounced it "Jackalin") and that I loved him. He took my hand, squeezed it, pulled himself up in the bed and said, "I love you, too." The look on his face was like, "Where have you been?" When I went to the hospital early the next morning he had just died.

I am so proud to have been Ben Hogan's niece, and I am so thankful to have had the chance to love someone and be loved by someone like my Uncle Ben.

Valerie Hogan was very protective of her husband. For much of his golfing career, she accompanied him on the road. Later in life, she was an unpaid counsel to her husband during his many years as a businessman, first with his golf-equipment company and later in his oil dealings. Valerie was not only protective of her husband's time, but his reputation as well, which occasionally meant keeping tabs on media coverage of her husband. **Dr. Jim Murphy,** *Hogan's personal physician, knew firsthand that Valerie ran a tight ship when it came to monitoring what was being reported and said about Ben:*

I really cared about him and we were close friends, so I would never say anything derogatory about him. I've been interviewed about Ben on numerous occasions by golf magazines and a lot of writers around here (Fort Worth), and I know at times how you can get quoted on things. Valerie was very paranoid to the point where things didn't even have to be derogatory for her to interpret it that way. Like one day I was talking to one of the writers and I said, "You know, he had such great concentration, you would think he could block out everything, it was almost like he was mesmerized with the situation." And she took the damnedest exception to that, even though to me that was a compliment—that a guy could concentrate that hard. But to her, it was a derogatory statement, as though he was (being referred to as) goofy rather than focused.

Dr. Murphy first met Ben Hogan when he joined Rivercrest Country Club in the 1950s:

There was an older bunch of outstanding businessmen, such as Marvin Leonard, that Ben used to play with at Rivercrest before Marvin built Shady Oaks. And as soon as Shady Oaks opened up, Marvin and many of his cronies quit playing at Rivercrest. Ben, of course, moved out there, although he had played a good bit at Colonial.

He basically played at Shady Oaks and practiced and had lunch there. When I first met him, he was fairly aloof. Ben was not a very warm and outgoing man, but he was always very civil. He had a brother-in-law, Dr. Ditto, over in Arlington who took care of Ben. After the accident, he used to go down to the Ochsner Clinic (in

New Orleans) because he had a bad shoulder and a bad knee. And I think Dr. Ditto kind of looked after his knees until maybe 1960 or 1965. Then I kind of took it from there.

Valerie's sister was married to Gordon Harriman, and Gordon and I played a lot of golf together. I think it was probably through Gordon and a kind of osmosis that I became Hogan's doctor. Other than his knee and his shoulder, he had very few problems. He was hospitalized once when he had some pretty severe indigestion, and he thought it might be his heart, but it didn't prove to be. Dr. Bobby Brown, a very close friend, checked his heart out, but Ben wasn't having any heart problems. Basically, he was having more marital problems than heart problems.

Ben had a little problem with alcohol. Sometimes it would spoil his disposition as the day went along and sometimes it would try to spoil his home life. He had appendicitis and a ruptured appendix back in the eighties, and he had a pretty stormy recovery. And then it was ten or twelve or fifteen years later when he had his cancer of the colon.

———⚮———

Dee Kelly, a prominent Fort Worth attorney and an avid golfer as well, became closely associated with Hogan over the last twenty years of Hogan's life. He also got to know Valerie well:

I did a lot of work for Ben and Valerie in the last years of his life, and the last year of her life. And I thought Valerie was the most dedicated wife I've ever seen in my life. He sacrificed a lot of things in life to be such a good golfer, and I think she wanted the world to know it. She was very supportive and important to him and very close. She followed him, traveled with him, and looked after him. She went with him to the British Open in 1953, when he was ready to come home before the tournament even started because he didn't like the hotel accommodations that had been assigned him. They didn't have a bathroom or any facilities for him to soak his legs. She had remembered that some company had offered him some other suitable accommodations, and so they moved over to there.

He was a delightful man. He was always extremely interesting to be around for dinners and that sort of thing. But he didn't like crowds.

The more **Dee Kelly** *got to know Hogan, the more he got to learn about what other people really thought about Hogan, and what he often discovered was a pleasant surprise. Such was the case at Ben Hogan's July 1997 funeral, with Kelly as one of the pallbearers:*

Sam Snead was a pallbearer at Hogan's funeral, too, which kind of surprised me. I always thought they were such protagonists. I couldn't imagine there would be a lot of deep feelings for each other. Valerie said that Snead told her at the funeral that he loved Ben, and Valerie told him, "He loved you too, Sam." And then Valerie said that Ben had always admired Sam and considered Sam as a champion. Hogan admired Snead's talent. And that was impressive. I felt those guys, having competed against each other for so long, probably would have a lot of resentment toward each other. Snead bragged about beating Hogan. But he told her that he loved Ben, and the feeling was mutual.

Ben and Valerie Hogan were gracious hosts as well, occasionally entertaining their closest friends, which included Fort Worth oilman **Tex Moncrief:**

Dinners at the Hogan home were nice. We'd have a drink of Crown Royal or something else before, and then we'd have plenty of wine. Valerie never did drink much. She would drink a little glass of wine. It could be the finest wine in the world, but she would put a couple of ice cubes in it. And I always said, "Valerie, golly, that's a great wine and you put a couple of ice cubes in it and ruined it." But anyway, she'd always drink that.

After Valerie died, they found three or four cases of white wine and a case of champagne, Dom Perignon, and I know damn well [that it was] what I had given Ben and Valerie over the years. By this time, the stuff was so damn old that it wasn't any good. With champagne, you're supposed to drink it in a year or two. And Ben had some wine out there that I'll guarantee is dated back almost to the sixties and the seventies. I'd give Ben and Valerie a case of wine and stuff because we were good friends and kind of exchanged gifts. But there were a couple of cases of imported wine, and I know damn well I gave those to them because you couldn't buy them around here. And damned if he hadn't left those wines. They didn't drink a lot, and then would probably drink a cheaper wine and say, "Well, maybe we'll save this for later," and then the old wines had just gone to nothing. They will turn to vinegar if you don't drink them.

The dinners where we would have good wine and all that were very good. Speaking about dinners, sometimes we'd go to the club or we might have a little party or maybe a little private tournament—not a club tournament—just where we might invite, say, twenty guys. We'd have about five foursomes maybe, and I remember years ago when we'd go to those little parties we'd like to get home fairly early. There was an old tune back then, you know, "Jambalaya on the Bayou." One night we were at this party and it was about over. I got up and said, "You know, boys, in the cool, cool, cool of the evening you kind of need to get home," and I said, "Good-bye Joe, we gotta go on the bayou. Good-bye Joe, we gotta go me-o-my-o and a filet gumbo. Son of a gun we'll have big fun . . ." and I looked over at Ben and he said in a low voice, ". . . on the Bayou." I had told Ben what I was gonna do. I was going to get up and sing this little ditty and when I got to that point he was supposed to say, "On the bayou." It brought the house down. From then on for years, whenever we would go to a party and I'd catch Ben's eye or he'd catch mine, I'd get up and start that song, and he'd come in and he knew what was coming, but I got a big kick out of that. It really was a signature duet, so to speak.

———

A man of few words, Hogan had a succinct way of getting a point across, loud and clear, as **Tex Moncrief** *points out:*

The worst thing that Ben could say about you or in describing something was "Nothing divided by nothing." You know, that's really nothing. If he wanted to describe a person or if you said something or got into an argument or if he thought you were losing or he didn't think you were right, he would say that is nothing divided by nothing.

———

Hogan also had a funny way of breaking the ice with strangers, or when he really had nothing else to say, but knew he needed to say something. **Marty Leonard** *explains:*

He had a sense of humor, no question about it. Of course he always pulled the "Hennie Bogan" thing on me. He did that more in his later years, you know. But he would always say that to you and that was just the way he handled some situations. I don't really know the origin of it, but I know he said it all the time. It was just a way, I guess, of relaxing or if he didn't know what else to say— you know, as an opening comment or something. And he would do that with a lot of people.

———

When Hennie Bogan wanted to get away from the golf course and cut it up with his buddies, he would cut bait. One such fishing pal was **Gene Smyers,** *who remembers experiencing life in the fast lane with his favorite legendary golfer:*

Ben enjoyed fishing. I went fishing with Ben several times. In fact, we floated Yellowstone.

One particular time we went down to the Leonards' place at Fairfield—Indian Creek. And we went with Mr. Baldridge, who was chairman of Champlin. Ben did not like to ride with anyone else. He was a good driver and he drove Mr. Baldridge's big, long Cadillac. I don't want to call it a limousine, but it was big.

We left fairly early one morning, and this was before they had the loop around Dallas. We were circling Dallas to intersect with Interstate 45, and Ben started pulling over. I asked what he was doing, and he said, "Well, there's an officer flashing his lights at me." So he pulled over, rolled the window down, and said, "Officer, what's the problem?"

"You're speeding."

"I was only driving forty-five."

"That's what I mean. The speed limit is thirty."

And Ben said, "I didn't see a sign."

The officer said, "May I have your license, please?"

Ben pulled his license out and didn't say anything. He just handed his license to the policeman. He already had the book out and was writing on the ticket. I was sitting in the left back seat and I'm watching. Suddenly, the officer stopped writing, looked in, and said, "Mr. Hogan, are you the golfer?"

"Well, I play golf, yeah."

"You're Mr. Hogan?"

At that, he just handed Ben his license back, folded up the ticket he had been writing, and put the book back in his pocket. And he said, "Mr. Hogan, the speed limit out here is thirty and that sign's kinda hard to see back there. May I ask where you gentlemen are going?"

"We're going fishing near Fairfield."

"You'll be coming back this way I assume."

"Yes sir, we sure will."

"Well, this is an area in which we find a lot of people speeding. I know that sign's a little bit hard to see both ways, so I encourage you to watch it coming back. I sure hope you gentlemen have a nice trip and a good day."

*While Hogan had great respect for the men in blue, he couldn't hide his disdain for hippies in blue jeans, as fellow golfer **Lionel Hebert** discovered one night in Massachusetts:*

One time we were playing a tournament in Worcester, Massachusetts, and Ben was there. It's not that big a town, but we found a restaurant one night that was about five blocks from our hotel. One day Hogan says, "Where you guys goin' to eat?" It was a nice lobster place, and the guy who ran the place really loved golf. He would get us seated without a wait. To get there, we had to walk by a post office. I was already at the restaurant when Val and Ben walked in and told us that they had walked by some hippies sitting on the steps of the post office, and that they had needled him and Valerie a little bit. So he asked the rest of us if we would mind walking with them back to the hotel, just in case those dudes showed up again. They weren't there, but you knew if they had been that he would have done something with us there with him.

There were rare occasions where someone who knew Hogan could "mess" with him a little bit, but you never messed with the

Hawk's rock candy, as **Gene Smyers** *points out, recalling a story Hogan once told him:*

I don't know whether this has ever been written about his caddie at the British Open (in 1953, Hogan's only British Open experience). Ben would buy rock candy. After the accident, he felt like he could gain some energy from the candy's sugar, and so he would put rock candy in his bag. But at about the midpoint of a practice round, he said, "I was out of rock candy. And I didn't understand that. This was a practice round. The same thing happened during the second practice round. I had been watching my caddie and he was eating more of that candy than I was. So that evening, I didn't say anything to him. I bought two bags of candy, gave them to him, and said, 'This bag's mine and that one's yours. Stay out of my candy.'"

Actually, he didn't have a problem about that. But Hogan said that during the first round, "The caddie was trying to talk to me, and he said if he couldn't talk to me he would talk to the gallery. So he was just yakking all the time. Finally, after the second round, I believe, I said, 'This is my office. I'm out here at work. We don't talk. You don't talk to me. You don't talk to the other players. You don't talk to the gallery. You don't talk to the other caddies. And you don't talk to the gallery. We're working.'" That's Hogan. That was the guy who gave Hogan the nickname "the Wee Icemon." Ben was very lavish in his praise of him.

The story has been told about asking him the greatest shot he ever had and he said, "Oh, I don't know. Maybe the shot I hit in the British Open. I had a one-stroke lead on the back nine and Peter Thomson was playing right behind me, and I hit a ball, and it was half in and half out of this little bunker and the bunker is flat. I couldn't tell if the ball was half on what grass there was or half on what sand there was. The pin's cut right against it, and it's not ten feet on. I'd never had this shot before. I didn't know how to hit it. I probably took twenty practice swings. And I looked back at the fairway and saw Peter Thomson, who smokes all the time." Of course, Ben did, too. He said, "All I could see was smoke, and I knew he was steaming because I'm up here taking practice swings trying to determine if I wanted to blast it or if I wanted to chip it. I finally determined how to hit it and I knocked it in the cup, and the match was all over. When that shot went in, I had a two-shot lead and knew he wasn't going to beat me."

———

Hogan was notorious for asking questions—lots of them, and all of them well thought out in his quest for knowledge and understanding. **Dr. Jim Murphy,** *Hogan's personal physician, recalls Hogan as a cooperative patient, but one who wanted to know everything he could about the x-rays, the prescriptions, and the various treatments:*

He would ask me medical questions as they related to himself. I looked at his x-rays and stuff when he had his knee and shoulder stuff. Because of the circulation in his legs from the accident, I think a knee replacement was just coming into vogue at the time, but they thought that the circulation in his legs was not adequate to risk the surgery. So he never did have that. Also, there were some degenerative changes in his shoulder. But that never seemed to be a big factor with him. His left knee was a lot more bothersome than his shoulder.

He had a pretty good brace that required constant change. And he would stiffen. He could be pretty sore, but he was certainly never a complainer. All he wanted was a full explanation about everything physical going on with him. He was a great patient, because he would do exactly what you told him to do. You know, most independent guys kind of do it the way they want. For those guys, you do it for them the way *they* want you to do it, but he was never that way. If you had a treatment for his problem, he might ask you why you do this and why you do that, but he would follow my directions absolutely to the T. That was the thing—he never hedged.

I don't think I ever ordered any fancy medicines for him. We'd just use Tylenol. At one time he was on an arthritis medicine that has since gone by the wayside and been replaced. He used a good bit of liniment and a good bit of heat, but he wasn't one who wanted codeine or analgesics. He was just pretty tough, I can tell you that. I can't remember him complaining much about pain. But I knew he was in a lot of pain. I could see him when his leg was so swollen from that accident: He just had a hard time walking. I don't know how he was ever able to compete, walking those eighteen holes. He was a plenty tough guy. Determined. And he was that way in every phase of his activities. He was very intent and he wanted everything to be perfect. He didn't have much sympathy for poor performance in any phase, whether it was in the oil industry or whether it was somebody taking care of his car.

Dr. Murphy *was not only Hogan's personal physician, he also became Byron Nelson's in the early 1970s, giving Murphy a patient duo unmatched in golf annals:*

I remember when Byron changed doctors. I'd already known him something like ten or fifteen years. He came out to the golf course at Shady Oaks and rode around on the scooter with me just kind of feeling me out. This was on a Wednesday, when I was playing. Byron's doctor had died. It was about 1970, and I had met him, but I didn't really know him. I was pretty flattered when he asked me if I would be his doctor.

Before Ben died, I had been talking to Byron every two or three days because he was interested to know how Ben was doing. They were friends, but not bosom buddies. So when Ben died I called him that morning and said that he had died. And I think somebody from New York called Byron and they had a little scoop in the paper that Hogan had died, and Byron's name was mentioned. And Valerie just never forgave him. She thought he was seeking publicity by getting the news out to the newspapers that Ben had died. And she got all hot and bothered. It never bothered Valerie's and my relationship, but it sure as hell bothered Byron and Valerie. This was just how paranoid she really was. And she got worse and worse as time went on. She misconstrued the meaning of things. Poor Valerie had a tough time with that.

Dr. Murphy *knew Hogan right up to the end, and it wasn't the most pleasant of times.*

After he had the (colon) surgery, I went by every week or two weeks—almost every week the last two years. We'd just shoot the bull, but you know he had Alzheimer's, and he couldn't remember anything. That was when Valerie wouldn't accept that. And you know his drinking didn't help. I think, basically, Ben was pretty much an unhappy guy. He was very successful and he was a good businessman. But it seemed to me that after he sold the golf company to AMF (in 1993), that he got more withdrawn and kind of lost interest in the golf clubs. Pretty much his whole life was centered around his friends at Shady Oaks.

---

*As far as **Marty Leonard** was concerned, Hogan's passing left her with some unfinished business:*

One of the things I'll always regret is that I was never able to get the two of them out to see my own golf facility out on I-30 (west of Fort Worth), which had Hogan prints all over the wall and is now owned by Family Golf. It was not easy to get him out, and you knew if it was too hot they couldn't do it. But we had it all set up one day, but something happened—I don't remember what—but they couldn't come, so I was disappointed. I had about a dozen of the prints of Jules Alexander photos he autographed for me out there. I tried never to ask him for a lot of things. After I was an adult and after my father was gone, everybody knew that we were friends and wanted to get stuff autographed for them. I was very, very careful about that. I just didn't do much of that.

You could have easily been swamped with that sort of thing. I had made the arrangement for Ben to get with Jules to come down here and meet him right here in Shady Oaks. I set that up so that he could get with him and visit with him, and he was nice enough to get me a set of those.

HOGAN, THE MASTER

He couldn't pull the trigger on his putts, even though he could hit the ball great. Literally, he looked like he was frozen.

—HALE IRWIN

Ben Hogan was not a natural-born thriller at golf. He battled a bad hook into his thirties, and he didn't win his first major until age thirty-four, at the 1946 PGA Championship. His golf career hit its stride in the mid-1940s only after he unlocked his game by, as he said, "digging it out of the ground," rebuilding his swing from the ground up. Hogan accomplished all this without the assistance of a swing guru. He spent thousands of hours grinding away on practice tees, becoming a master with every club. Each club in his bag became an extension of the man as he became one of the greatest shotmakers in golf history. Hogan was a *maestro* as much as he was a master.

When professional golfers rate one another, they typically use one of two criteria—shotmaking and ballstriking. There is a difference. Great ballstrikers get the maximum physical performance out of their clubs, crisply striking shots that rarely stray from desired paths of ball flight. Great shotmakers, on the other hand, are right-brain creative, able to visualize shots others can't see. They can shape shots in a variety of directions and extricate themselves from all sorts of circumstances. Jack Nicklaus and Bobby Jones were brilliant ballstrikers. Seve Ballesteros and Lee Trevino are classic shotmakers. Hogan was both. He was a wonderful ballstriker and perhaps an even better shotmaker. He understood the intricacies of engineering a great ballstriking swing, yet he practiced so much that he knew well what every club could do and under whatever situations were thrown at him.

Hogan was peerless when it came to exercising his uncanny ability to focus—to block out all distractions and emotions that could interfere with his well-rounded game. Had it not been for putting woes after the age of forty, which went from bad to worse as he aged, Hogan likely would have won one or two PGA Tour events a year into his fifties, maybe even his sixties. Yet it didn't take a sanctioned tournament to get his juices flowing. Hogan could be just as stoic and steely in a "fun" game of golf, whether it be for a $25 payoff in a game of "Points" or a round of $50 birdies. Whatever secrets Hogan kept to himself, there was always someone, even a Nick Faldo, who would occasionally detour through Fort Worth in search of an audience with Hogan and perhaps a chance to learn a new swing key that would crank their own game up to another level. When the master talked, people listened, even if it was just a curt "You're away" out on the golf course.

Hogan won four official U.S. Opens and narrowly missed winning at least three others, most notably the 1955, 1956, and 1960 Opens, ultimately won by Jack Fleck, Cary Middlecoff, and Arnold Palmer, respectively. Still, Hogan believed he actually won more than four Opens, as his attorney **Dee Kelly** *points out:*

What was meaningful to Ben was that he believed he won five Opens, and he went to his dying day believing he had won five, including the Hale America Open (in 1942).

—

The 1960 U.S. Open at Cherry Hills in Colorado was probably the most memorable of the U.S. Opens that Hogan had a chance to win but he didn't. That was the year that two and a half generations of legendary golfers collided, with Palmer coming from behind to hold off the likes of Hogan and Jack Nicklaus to win. Hogan, forty-seven at the time, was in close contention when he got to the seventeenth hole. Figuring he needed a birdie at the par-five hole fronted by a moat, Hogan tried to stick his approach as close to the hole as he could, only for the ball to hit almost hole-high and then suck back into the water, knocking Hogan out of the running. Hogan roundtable companion **Gene Smyers** *tells the story of what was going through Hogan's mind as he was setting up the shot:*

There's been a lot of comments about him hitting the ball into the water on seventeen at Cherry Hill in 1960. I later heard him talk about this a number of times. He said, "This green had an elevation in it on the front of the green, and the pin was at the very front. And it was a two-tiered green. I knew if I hit the ball above, there

All-told, Hogan won four official U.S. Open titles. This million-dollar smile accompanies his trophy for his victory in the 1951 Open at Oakland Hills, for his third career Open championship. (AP/Wide World Photos)

would be no way to make that putt. I hit a wedge and I thought the ball was absolutely perfect. And it hit right on the front and backed off into the water. I didn't miss the shot. Maybe I should have hit it three feet farther, but I don't have three feet in my wedge—I can't gauge that distance that closely. I thought I hit that ball perfect."

---

*In the 1955 Open at Olympic, Jack Fleck beat Hogan in a Monday playoff. As Hogan told **Smyers,** it just wasn't his tournament to win:*

He never spoke about Fleck in a disparaging way. He said that on the eighteenth hole at Olympic, he (Fleck) hit a drive so wide over the fairway, it was over in the rough. "Previously, the rough had been such that he would have done well just to get the ball out," he said. "But by this time, the gallery had walked and trampled it down and he said it was just as flat as this tabletop (Smyers is seated at their Shady Oaks table). It's just flat. And Fleck hit an iron in, I don't know, six or eight feet, and made the birdie. It just seemed like I was almost destined not to win. I have no other explanation for it."

---

*One of the young spectators who saw Hogan play in the 1960 U.S. Open was **Hale Irwin,** who, like Hogan, was a classic grinder and someone who would go on to win three U.S. Opens himself:*

I saw him play twice, including once when he played in the 1960 U.S. Open at Cherry Hills. The other time, I think in 1967, was when I was playing at Champions (in the Houston Open)—one of four collegians invited that year to play in the event. I went out and watched him play a few holes with Palmer. I remember how his shots seemed kind of lasered. They'd go out to a certain point then hook back into the pin. Still, although we tend to put him on a pedestal, there are hundreds of pictures of him hitting out of bunkers, too. So he did miss some shots.

I was fifteen in 1960 when I saw him play in the '60 Open at Cherry Hills. That was the year Tommy Bolt threw his driver into the water. I went down on the practice days because I couldn't get a ticket for the tournament itself, probably because it was too expensive. I went just one day and can remember snippets, such as one time on the fourth green, where Hogan stood over a three-foot putt for what must have been minutes. It was almost like he was a statue, which was the problem Hogan came to. He couldn't pull the trigger on his putts, even though he could hit the ball great. Literally, he looked like he was frozen. It was uncomfortable for me— an embarrassing moment—I thought a pigeon was going to come land on him. But I wasn't so enamored of Hogan to where I held him in any greater esteem than I did Nicklaus or Palmer, because I was really more concerned with how I was playing myself.

Most great golfers are closely associated with one of the four major tournaments, and Hogan was most closely associated with the U.S. Open. But when golfers turned up for the 1963 Open to be played that year at the Country Club outside Boston, Hogan was nowhere to be seen. He hadn't earned a spot in the field, and the USGA had made no special provisions to invite Hogan. **Lionel Hebert** *was among those golfers who would have preferred an Open with Hogan in it rather than one without him:*

There was one year, 1963, that we were playing the U.S. Open at the Country Club in Boston, but Hogan wasn't in the field. No one could understand why Hogan hadn't been invited. Heck, the man had won the Open four times. So I called a friend of mine on the USGA's board, Hord Hardin (the future Masters Tournament chairman) and asked him about it. He said, "We've got to make room for new players and don't have room for all of the past Open champions." But Hord started thinking about it and the next year at Congressional they offered Hogan a spot in the Open field. All the players knew it was a feather in our cap any time we had Hogan's name in the field, even if he didn't win.

Hogan's niece, **Jacqueline Hogan Towery,** *learned about her uncle's on-course demeanor and the accompanying rules of etiquette at an early age:*

Number One Rule: Never, ever talk to Uncle Ben when he was on the golf course—not anywhere. Golf was his business, the way he made a living, and that's why he concentrated so hard that he shut out everyone and everything else when he was playing. It was always fun to be in the gallery and listen to what people had to say about Ben. They didn't know who I was, and I heard a lot . . . always good. People respected him very much and admired his dedication.

One day a very special thing happened to me. I was walking down the fifteenth fairway during the Colonial National Invitation Tournament. This was when the gallery followed the players down the fairway, and of course, I was following Uncle Ben as closely as I could. I saw him out of the corner of my eye, but I kept walking, eyes straight ahead, as I had been told. He saw me and said, "Well, hello, Jacqueline. How are you?" I was so stunned I could hardly speak, but I finally managed, "Fine, Uncle Ben." That was the only time of which I am aware that he ever spoke to anyone during a tournament round, including me, ever again.

One of golf's other great Bens, **Ben Crenshaw,** *is a student of golf history. He understands and appreciates Hogan's place in history as well as anyone can:*

Although Hogan will always be remembered as arguably the finest ballstriker ever, in my opinion his quick, analytical mind was probably his strongest personality trait as a champion golfer. He was a bit of a loner and was actually somewhat shy, but he found a great passion and love for the solitude of golf and its unique challenge.

The power of his mind made Hogan a great field mar-

A Hogan family get-together for Christmas in the early 1940s: (left to right)
Royal Hogan and his wife, Margaret; B. B. and PaPa Duncan (Margaret
Hogan's parents), Jacque Hogan (Royal's daughter; Ben's niece, with doll);
Princess Ditto (Ben and Royal's sister); Valerie and Ben Hogan (then in the
Army Air Corps); and Clara "Mama" Hogan. (Photograph provided courtesy
of Jacqueline Hogan Towery)

shal on the golf course. He could analyze (very rapidly)
how to play a course, and the management of his skills
and sticking to a game plan were always hallmarks of his
game. . . .

Hogan's exploits and tournament wins are well
chronicled and are laid down in hard numbers, but what
remains burned into all our memories is the way he
played and won them. He once was asked about today's
professionals, who rely heavily on yardage books in
choosing a club and shot. Hogan, who preferred to play

by observation, analysis, and feel, said simply, "It would deprive me the pleasure of a well-executed shot."[2]

Hogan had a superhuman ability to tune out thoughts and other distractions during a round of golf, which served him especially well during major championships. Shady Oaks club pro **Mike Wright** *remembers a conversation he once had with Hogan on that specific issue, a conversation in which Hogan made it sound like that proper focus was as simple as utilizing one's common sense:*

I sat and talked to him a lot about golf. I've heard him talk a lot about business. I never had a lot of one-on-one. I talked to him about the state of the industry. We talked about golf-shop merchandising. We talked about equipment. We talked about the golf swing and how people interpret the golf swing. We talked about course management.

He was always very direct—very intelligent about any subject. And if he didn't know about the subject, he would ask very intelligent questions. Everything he said was very, very well thought through. He teased and joked, but nothing was ever said just off the cuff in a serious conversation. You asked him a question and he answered it sincerely.

One time we talked about how he could possibly maintain focus on the golf course like he did. How did he train himself to do that? And he said, "Well, Mike, you're playing golf, what else could you be thinking about?" And he obviously knew that was a sharper answer than what I had been looking for. But I understood what he was saying, and he added, "Let me make it more clear. If you are prepared to play, you don't have time to have anything else on your mind at all. Playing a golf course or tournament golf is like preparing for an exam. If you are willing, you can know every single potential question that might be asked on that exam. As an example, you know where the flag may be, you know where the tees may be, you know how the wind may blow. If you are willing to prepare and study that golf course and prepare your swing to match the circumstances you may face, that's how you maintain focus. There is so much going on that you won't have time to get distracted. Say you've got a tournament coming up. Are you willing to put in the time to figure out everything that can be asked and then prepare yourself physically to achieve that?"

I had never thought about golf that way, where if you anticipate every possible question that can be asked, you spend time researching the answers, memorizing them or whatever, and once you do that, really, there is no more anxiety. Anxiety is the fear of the unknown or dealing with the predicament on a golf course you're not ready for. Say you're hitting to the right and it goes through your mind that "now that I'm here, oh my God, everything looks different. I've got a different approach." You panic. That's how he could come up with the story of when he would leave the six- or seven-iron out of his bag at Champions (in Houston) or something like that.

Senior PGA Tour golfer **Gene Littler,** the 1961 U.S. Open champion, was more succinct in discussing Hogan's tunnel

*vision. Littler often has been called "Gene, the Machine,"
although that was a nickname that he would just as soon confer
on Hogan:*

He was very quiet. He was just kind of the mechanical
man—no one ever hit it any straighter than he did. It
was fun watching him play because everything just went
that way. (Littler points straight ahead.)

⊶⊷

*Speaking of mechanical men, let's not forget Nick Faldo, the
three-time Masters winner and three-time British Open champion,
who was at one time known as "Robogolfer." The story
has often been told of how Hogan allegedly snubbed Faldo when
the latter paid a visit to Hogan in Fort Worth, although Hogan
roundtable club member **Bob Wynne** says the popular story is
flawed, that in fact Hogan was friendly and accommodating
with Faldo:*

On that day I was not aware that Faldo was coming for
lunch and we were looking out, facing the eighteenth
hole, and I said, "That looks like Nick Faldo." Mr. Hogan
never said a word. Faldo came in the back door and came
right to the table, introduced himself, and sat right next
to Mr. Hogan. I heard the whole conversation. Later on
in the newspaper, it was reported that Hogan stone-
walled Faldo that day. That was their line, anyway. But
that did not happen, and I know this because I was right
there. The member who had been quoted had not been
there—he had been at a different table across the room.
It was someone who had become hacked off by Mr.
Hogan because of a previous incident.

What did happen was we had lunch and the four or five of us were involved in conversation. At one point after lunch, Faldo said, "I wonder if you would go up on the range with me because I want to hit some balls." He wanted Hogan to come watch because he was having a little problem. Hogan didn't immediately respond to him. He just sat there for a while, and then said, "No, I found out when I work these things out myself, they stay with me longer and they're better," or something to that effect. But he was nice about it; there wasn't anything abrupt like "I won't go up there." Then Ben said to Faldo, "When you get through, come back." So Faldo went up there and hit some balls, but not for very long, and then he came back. They visited for a while, it was all very cordial, and then Faldo's group left. David Hueber took him to the airport, then came back, and he and I played golf. David told me that Faldo was quite happy with how everything went.

<hr />

Hogan, however, could be harsh to some extent to other highly skilled golfers, as **Arnold Palmer** *discovered leading up to the 1958 Masters:*

My pal Dow Finsterwald had arranged for us to team up and play with Ben Hogan and Jackie Burke in a practice round. After my bone-wearying midnight drive across South Carolina (to say nothing of the deflation I felt at losing the playoff [at the Azalea Open in Wilmington, Delaware]), I went out on the course that morning and played abysmally. I felt doubly bad that Dow had to carry us both—he played brilliantly and we collected $35 apiece off the wager. A little while afterward, as we were changing in the club locker room, I heard Ben Hogan remark to Jackie, "Tell me something, Jackie. How the hell did Palmer get an invitation to the Masters?"

That really stung me. I'll never know if Hogan knew I overheard the comment. But he certainly was aware that I was nearby and could have overheard it. I knew he was probably the most precise shotmaker who ever played the game and no particular fan of my style of play, having once said of my game, "Palmer's swing might work for him, but no one else should try it." In any event, the question burned me up and set my mind on showing him why the hell I'd been invited to the Masters. So perhaps I owe Ben a tip of the cap for helping me focus my mind on my business the way Pap always insisted I would have to in order to win a major golf tournament."[3] (Palmer went on to win the 1958 Masters.)

Ironically, that same year at Augusta, Hogan paid another young, up-and-coming star golfer with the ultimate compliment by inviting him to be his partner in a friendly practice round against rival Sam Snead and another golfer. Hogan's young man of the moment was none other than current CBS-TV golf analyst **Ken Venturi,** *who says:*

We played a practice round at the Masters. And I said, "Boy, Ben, I sure enjoyed playing with you. It's just great." And he said, "You will always play with me."

We were upstairs having lunch one day, and Sam Snead came in there when all the players were having lunch. I was down at the end of the table and Ben was right near the door, and Sam comes in and says, "You got a game, Ben?"

"No."

"You want a game?"

"Yeah."

"Who you got?"

I was about six guys down on the table, and Ben says, "I'll take Venturi and play anybody in the world." Sam took a long look and said, "I can find a better game than that," and he walked off. I couldn't look up. I was sitting next to (Mike) Souchak and I damn near choked my food down. I remember that like it was yesterday. Souchak gave me a shot in the ribs, and I said, "Don't touch me. Don't get near me."

—⊷∭⊷—

Sam "the Slammer" Snead took over the chore of being the other half of a Hogan rivalry after Byron Nelson retired, although Snead had had an eye on Hogan's golfing habits for many years, as he told this author in a 1989 Fort Worth Star-Telegram *interview:*

He changed his game around, looking for a swing that would repeat. All great golfers have a different look and swing, but all look alike at the point of contact. Ben eventually shortened his swing, yet finished so high on his follow-through . . . He hit a lot of (practice) balls. He had the ability and the desire—all your better players have that. Most guys on tour go two or three years and then fade into the sunset. The good ones always come back.

I know the mannerisms of all these guys. I cataloged people. I knew how they held their hands, if they limped, whether or not they twitched. With Ben, it was not showing an expression. He was a card dealer at one time, and that's where he got that stone face. You couldn't tell if he was winning or losing. That's also where he got his patience . . . One time we were playing in a team championship (at Inverness, Ohio). Jimmy Demaret had just started playing cards when Ben came over, took the cards out of his hands, and said, "No card playing." He knew you could get too high or too low from playing cards.

———

Former PGA Tour golfer **Mason Rudolph** *first saw the masterful Hogan at work when they played an exhibition round together in 1951 in Jackson, Tennessee. Rudolph, then seventeen, had just won the National Junior Championship and ended up "beating" Hogan that day by one shot, 70 to 71. Later, after turning professional, Rudolph counted seven times that he was paired with Hogan in PGA Tour events. One of those occasions was a Colonial Tournament in Fort Worth, where Rudolph got a brief glimpse of another side of Hogan—the sunny side:*

I think it was one of his last competitive rounds. I was a little jumpy teeing off with him, being in a threesome with him and Bob Rosburg. We played the opening par-five hole and made par on that. The second hole was a short par-four, dogleg left to right and downwind. Hogan drove it into the right fairway bunker. Rosburg was in the left rough, and I drove it right down the center, so I was feeling a little better. I mean, we had five thousand people following us.

Hogan hit it from there into another bunker up by the green, and Rosburg flew it over the green into high grass. The wind was blowing so hard behind us, and the pin was tucked in behind that bunker. So I used a sand wedge. I knew I couldn't stop it, so I just hit it to the center part of the green, leaving me about a twenty-footer. Rossie tried to run it up there, but it got caught up in the rough. So then he goes and chips it in for a four. Hogan gets in the bunker and hits it, but leaves it in there. Hogan then holes *his* out for a four. I putt three feet by and miss it coming back, finishing with a bogey after I had been in the best shape of the three to get a birdie there. We're walking to the next hole and now I'm a nervous wreck. I'm really shook. Hogan comes up behind me and says, "Mason, you don't know how to play that hole, do you?" and he starts grinning. That kind of loosened me up. At the time, I was playing his equipment, but he still wouldn't say much during his round.

———

*Hogan won his hometown Colonial tournament five times, the last time in 1959 at age forty-six, and somewhere in the middle of all that became part of an answer to fellow Texan **Rocky Thompson**'s favorite golf trivia question. Note, by the way, how Thompson pays homage to both Hogan's ballstriking and shotmaking abilities:*

I was on the fourteenth tee at Colonial on a Saturday, where I had been paired with Doug Sanders and Tommy Bolt. They had both withdrawn during the round, so now I'm a onesome. I call a PGA Tour official and he didn't have a clue what to do. So then I called for the head guy, and he said, "Just join the group behind you." The group behind me was Bob Goalby, Chi Chi Rodriguez, and *Mr.-Ben-Hogan-the-greatest-shotmaker-who-has-ever-lived*. And here's Rocky Thompson—he had never heard of me from Joe Schmuck. So on that first hole with us together, the fourteenth, I hit it in the rough and chop it out. I'm forty yards short of this par-four in two, then pitch it up twenty feet, make the putt, and give it a little James Brown knee-pop. True story, and Bob Goalby tells it all the time. So Hogan goes over to Goalby and says, "Who is this son of a bitch?" That's the all-time greatest sports trivia question: What pro on the PGA Tour in one eighteen-hole round played golf with Tommy Bolt, Doug Sanders, Ben Hogan, Chi Chi Rodriguez, and Bob Goalby. It's a riddle on how the heck it could ever happen.

The next time I got paired with him was again on a Saturday at Colonial. I got paired with him and Tom Weiskopf. Now how do you like that? Here you've got *Hogan-the-greatest-shotmaker-who-has-ever-lived*, and you've got Tom Weiskopf, the most majestic ballstriker who has ever lived—the high, towering, 280-yard drives that carry and draw a hair if he wants. Anyway, I'm paired with those two guys, and Hogan bogeys the first two holes—the easiest two holes on the course. For the next sixteen holes, however, his golf ball never left the pin. He never missed one shot because he is the *greatest-ballstriker-who-has-ever-lived*. And he shot three under those last sixteen holes for a 69 and passed something like twenty guys and that was very memorable. I can remember that like yesterday. And he talked! He mostly talked to his caddie, and he talked to us, too. He was fun

to play with. In fact it was wonderful to play with him
and to watch him.

———

*Hogan not only frowned on showboating, he didn't take kindly
to other golfers who would try to bend the rules, even when it
involved hard-to-monitor specs regarding golf equipment.*
Tommy Jacobs *can't help but laugh as he fondly remembers
one such incident:*

I think it was in 1959, and I was in the barbershop at
Colonial with Ernie Vossler, a mutual friend who lived
near the golf course. I had just met Ben, but had never
played golf with him. Ben comes walking into the barbershop, comes up to me, and says, "You gotta game?" I
ended up playing three straight days with him and
Tommy Bolt. They had a lot of banter going back and
forth the whole time, and I just listened. I remember that
the greens were pretty firm then and Ben noticed that
Tommy's ball was stopping pretty well on the green with
his approach shots. Finally, Ben took one of the irons out
of Tommy's hands and ran his hand across the clubface.
Right away he could feel where someone had worked on
Tommy's grooves, raising the top portion of the grooves
just enough so that they would protrude forward and add
more bite to the ball. When Ben took Tommy's club,
Tommy goes, "Ahhh, Ben," and Hogan goes, "Don't give
me that 'Ahhh, Ben,' stuff. Take these clubs down to my
factory and get the faces smoothed down the way they
should be. You can bet that if I'm going to play in this
tournament, you won't be playing with these irons."
Back then, the rules about altering clubs weren't as

strictly enforced, but Ben wasn't going to put up with it. And he didn't.

———

Praise for other golfers did not spill out of Hogan's mouth easily, if at all. **Tommy Jacobs,** *about twenty years younger than Hogan, found that out during his early years on the PGA Tour:*

One time after playing a tournament round with Ben at Colonial, we were in the locker room and I overheard Ben being interviewed by the media. By then, Ben only gave interviews in the locker room instead of going to the press room like the other golfers did. Someone asked him about the young fella that had been playing with him that day—me—and all Ben said was, "Two hacks, one slash, and a putt equals four," and that was it. In other words, I had had a scrambling round.

———

Senior PGA Tour golfer **Jim Ferree,** *who got to know Hogan through his father, a former pro at Pinehurst, remembers Hogan's being almost perfect from tee to green but with a severe liability on the green that got worse over time:*

I came on tour in 1955, about the time Hogan was starting to cut way back on his schedule. I played with him in Houston, in Philadelphia, and several times in Fort Worth. Ernie Vossler was a good friend of mine and a member at Colonial, and with Ben being a member there, too, and a friend of Ernie's, I got to play with Hogan several times.

Ben and I got along okay. I never asked for a practice round. Gardner Dickinson, and Jay and Lionel Hebert were close friends, too, so we would hang around together and every now and then Ben would ask us to play. He hit it very well. He drove his ball in the fairway and reasonably long for that day and time. And his iron play was extremely precise. At one time he had been an outstanding putter, but that went away.

I distinctly remember one tournament round when he, Mike Souchak, and I were paired together for the last day at an event in Philadelphia. I wasn't playing particularly well, driving it in the rough some and hitting some scratchy-looking irons. Souchak was playing pretty well, and Ben was playing his normal beautiful game. But I don't think he could see well by then, because he would hit the prettiest-looking shots and they would fall short of the green. Keep in mind, too, that we didn't have yardages then the same as we do now.

On the last hole, I hooked my drive into the left rough, Souchak hit into the right rough, and Hogan hit his tee shot right down the middle. Souchak and I both missed the green with our second shots. Ben hit his second shot right at the pin, but it went just over the flag to the back fringe. He then stubbed his next shot only about six feet, leaving him a fifteen-foot downhill putt. From there, he three-putted for a double-bogey six while Mike and I both made our putts for pars, and I think we all ended up shooting 73. That goes to show how misleading scores can sometimes be because Hogan had played so much better (tee to green) than either of us.

Golfing opponents winced when they saw Hogan badly miss makable putts late in his career, and the view wasn't any better for Hogan's spectating friends, such as **Dr. Jim Murphy:**

In the later competitive days, when he'd play out there at Colonial in the sixties, he got to where he couldn't get the damn putter back. I went out there a number of times when they had that tournament dinner on Wednesday with the past winners there, and I guess I went a half a dozen times with Ben, Valerie, and Sara, who was Valerie's sister. We were just very close friends. And Ben was a pretty damn good speaker.

The thing that really broke my heart was to see him try to hit that three-foot putt. He couldn't get the putter back and he would miss about 50 percent of them. He had been a hell of a good putter in his prime. He'd stand over that putt and sometimes walk away and get back over it, and he just had the blind stares. And then finally he'd just jab it. They call it the yips, but he could just not get the putter blade back. He talked to everybody he could think of about it. He tried tranquilizers, and if I'm not mistaken, I think he even tried hypnosis. He certainly knew he had a problem. I was the one who said, "Maybe you could try a little tranquilizer," but it was no more than that. As I recall, I never ordered anything for him. You know, that's the height of humiliation. And I think in a sense it was pretty much why he didn't play in that Legends of Golf tournament down at Austin. I think he and Jimmy Demaret were going to play or thought about playing. But I think he backed out.

He didn't seem to have much trouble with the putter when he was playing (for recreation). I remember one

Hogan in the twilight of his competitive career, playing in the 1970 Westchester Classic, while showing it's possible to puff and swing at the same time. (Jules Alexander photo)

day he shot his age—he shot a 64 when he was sixty-five (in the late 1970s). And he wasn't having trouble with the putter at that time.

It is commonly believed that Hogan played his last competitive round in the Houston Open at Champions Golf Club in 1971, with playing partners **Charles Coody** *and Kermit Zarley unwittingly witnessing history when Hogan pulled out in the middle of a round after reaggravating a knee injury. Coody recalls that fateful day, although Zarley points out that Hogan did indeed play in one more tour event after that, at Westchester, at the request of Hogan friend John Schlee (Hogan would play only one round before withdrawing). Coody recalls that sad, earlier day at Champions:*

87

I played with him during his last competitive round, at Houston in 1971. The third member of the group was Kermit Zarley. Ben didn't have a good day. He hit the ball down in the ravine on the fourth hole. He tried to go down and play it, but turned his knee. Later he hit a shot fat on the twelfth hole, a par-three, and it hit a bank and came back into the water. He just looked at me and said, "I'm sorry, but I just can't go." And he gave his card to me and said, "I'll see ya." I understood. At that time, he had higher standards than anyone else did. I don't think he quit just because he was playing bad—I think he quit because he just wasn't physically able to play. His ability to strike the ball, even into his late fifties, was phenomenal. It was his short game, the putting, that kept him from playing more than he did. He definitely had the malady called the yips. Everything would just start shaking when he tried to putt.

By the time the first Legends of Golf Tournament was contested in 1978, Hogan was already past his sixty-fifth birthday, his competitive game almost seven years in mothballs. One story suggests that Jimmy Demaret and Hogan were set to team up in the two-man event, only for Hogan to decide against it. People close to Hogan believed he could have been a competitive senior golfer in his sixties and even into his seventies—if he could have continued to putt. At least, this is how attorney-friend **Dee Kelly** *sees it:*

He wouldn't play competitive golf in his later years because he couldn't play at the high level of perfection that he required of himself. And that's why he didn't get involved in the Legends of Golf Tournament and that kind of thing, even though he could play better golf than most of the other guys out there. Arnold Palmer will probably play golf until he's eighty, as long as he can make appearances—and (Jack) Nicklaus is still trying to play, too—but that just wasn't Hogan. His trouble was putting, and I think his nerves just got to him in the latter part of life. Ben smoked a lot, and I always thought that had a lot to do with it. That's an uneducated guess, but I suspect that's it.

Ben could have made a small fortune if he had played golf in some exhibitions with some of those other legends like Sam Snead. Even when he was seventy years old, he was as good as anybody in the world, but he couldn't putt as well. But he could sure hit the ball.

Although retired from tournament golf for the last twenty-five years of his life, Hogan would rarely turn down a friendly bet with his golfing buddies at Rivercrest and Shady Oaks. Longtime friend **Gene Smyers** *remembers that it was possible to beat Hogan—once:*

I met him at Rivercrest back in the fifties. I had the unusual experience of beating him the first time I played him. We had a foursome and Ben would never give anybody strokes. We played the first hole and I told him, "Mr. Hogan, we both parred the first hole, so I'll just play you for five dollars in an automatic two-down." I birdied nine and eighteen, and I won fifty dollars after he had pressed to get even on both nine and eighteen. And I would guess next time he beat me, costing me ten times that. At one point I was playing golf with Hogan once or twice a week for two or three months, and after a while I told him I didn't believe I could beat him (again).

Playing with him was interesting. One afternoon we'd teed off, and Ben was playing behind us in a two-some with someone. We saw him right behind us, so we invited him to come on and he hit his second shot in the cup for a 2 on number one. And I made some comment about it, and he said, "Well, you know, you can't birdie them all unless you birdie the first one." But he had made an eagle. I think Ben's idea of a perfect round of golf would have been to make eighteen birdies. And he didn't think that was impossible, just unlikely. But he had lofty goals. The stories that are well known about him have been told and probably embellished on, but he enjoyed practicing in a way that I just marveled at. And he was very faithful with it.

---

*Many golf experts will argue that Hogan was the world's great-est golfer of the twentieth century. Hogan's niece, **Jacqueline Hogan Towery,** makes a case that Hogan might not even have been the best golfer in the family. That's because Royal Hogan—Jacque's father and Ben's older brother—was an accomplished golfer in his own right:*

My dad, Royal Hogan, was no slouch as a golfer. He dominated the amateur golf scene in Fort Worth for a number of years. He won the Colonial Country Club member championship so many years straight that they finally decided not to allow him to enter anymore. And in the many times that Daddy played with Ben, Daddy won more often than Ben. I recently had an opportunity to visit with Lee Trevino in Dallas, and he asked me if I had any of Ben's clubs. I said no, but I had some of my father's clubs. I told him that I understood the sweet spot to be about the size of a pinhead, and Lee said, "I'm dead!"

—————

One of Hogan's favorite friendly games was "Points," and **Tommy Jacobs** *remembers how Hogan would always write the rules:*

I played about a dozen practice rounds with him over the years, but we really didn't talk about much because his mind was so much in his game. I don't know why, but I never played well during those practice rounds with him. One thing about playing with him is that you always had to play his game, and his favorite game was Points. Here's how it worked: If you missed a fairway with a shot, you got one point tacked on. It was two points for missing a green. The guy with the fewest points at the end of the round was the winner. I remember that I always had something like twenty-one or twenty-two points and Ben would have about half that. One time in particular, I remember finishing with plus-twenty-four and Ben had plus-eleven, and we were playing a dollar a point. I said, "Okay, Ben, I guess I owe you thirteen dollars." No big amount. But he says, "No, that's not the way we do it. The winner pays himself and you owe me for the total that you missed (not the difference)." I said, "Okay, Ben, if that's how you want to play it." The point of this game was fairways and greens, which is the name of the game in major championships.

Tex Moncrief played a number of friendly games with Hogan over the years, as did his own father before him:

I played a good number of rounds with Ben. So did my dad, and my dad was a very good golfer, a low handicapper. When Ben was right at the top of his game, sometime in the fifties, Hogan played my dad one day at Colonial. They were getting a little bit antagonistic with each other and bragging, and my dad beat him in an eighteen-hole match. Ben told me many times that he had never gotten over that.

Another time in the early eighties, we were playing golf at Shady Oaks. We had ourselves a foursome, and Ben joined us on the back side. We got around to the twelfth hole, which is a par-three. We were at the back tees when Ben was with us, so it was a couple hundred yards. We had a game out there we played a lot of times where you play fifty dollars on a birdie—"Twenty-five dollars I do and twenty-five dollars you don't." It's a total of fifty dollars. So I was back there getting ready to hit my drive. It may have been a little over two hundred, but I was hitting a driver. And I said, "Ben, you want fifty dollars on a birdie?" He knew what the game was. Of course, old Ben would just stare you down and wouldn't say a damn thing for what seemed like forever. Finally, he said, "Sure I'll take fifty . . . I'll take fifty thousand." I said,

"Ben, I just wanted a friendly little bet. I didn't want to get to gambling or anything."

So I knocked my drive onto the green, about twenty feet from the hole. Ben was a little outside of me. When Ben missed his putt and I made mine for a deuce, he owed me fifty dollars. Well, we went on playing and there was the usual little banter but not much talking with Hogan. In fact, I don't remember him saying anything. We got around to the sixteenth hole, which is another par-three. I teed my ball up and was getting ready to hit, when I heard somebody clearing his throat—Hogan. He said, "What about fifty here?" And I said, "Of course, Ben. I thought you had disappeared. I didn't know you were still around." Well, anyway, I knocked the ball up there about ten or twelve feet from the cup, but I did have a sidehill putt. Well, old Ben looked like he really concentrated, and sure enough he knocked one up there about three feet from the hole. I missed my putt and Ben made his. He never said another dang word. But that kind of shows you the way Ben was. That's the damn truth and I never will forget it.

He never played every day with us or anything like that. But we used to have a swing game out there where two people would take what we called "the swing" and those two people would play every other pair. There might be, say, sixteen or eighteen people there. If two people had the swing, they would play every other twosome. You might have twenty or thirty bets going on, and we'd play a fifty-dollar bet on each twosome. It was a pretty damn big game. The people that had the swing might win or lose two or three thousand dollars or more.

Ben did play in those games a few times. But with his

being a scratch player or a plus-1 or a plus-2, it was hard for him to win because a lot of us had handicaps and we'd make birdies. One day we must have had a couple dozen people out there after a Shady Oaks tournament. It was on Sunday and Ben decided to take the swing with a guy named Earl Baldridge. Ben went out that morning and got the greenskeeper, and he moved all the tees back for the amateurs—not to the back tees but as far back as he could get without being too bad. And he set all the pins in places that were very difficult for an amateur to hit at. And he and old Baldridge won several thousand dollars that day. And we call that the day of the big fug. He really put it to us. But nobody liked it and we never had Ben in the swing again.

---

*Hogan was not only a master at playing golf, he was a master at understanding it. That meant keeping up with what was going on in the golf world even when he was no longer really an integral part of it. Golfer **Tom Byrum** remembers how Hogan was always full of surprises when it came to contemporary golf knowledge:*

One day I was having lunch with him at the big round-table, joined by some other members who would come and go. A member came along, sat down, and started to talk about how Greg Norman was making a million dollars on the tour in official money. He asked Hogan if he could believe someone could make a million dollars on the tour. Hogan said yes and that, in fact, Norman was probably making that much off the tour in endorsements, too. The member was quiet for a minute and asked

Hogan, "Are you sure about that, Ben?" Hogan paused for a long time before answering. When he did, he asked the member what he did for a living. He replied, "Ben, you know I sell cars." And Hogan said, "That's right. You sell cars for a living." Hogan then said, "I don't know a damn thing about selling cars." After another pause, Hogan said, "But I do know golf, and when I tell you someone is making a million dollars playing golf, he's making a million dollars playing golf!!" Needless to say, that was the end of most of the conversation around the table.

———

*No discussion of Hogan's golfing prowess would be complete without discussing his willingness to practice for hours on end. Even after he had quit playing rounds of golf, Hogan could often be found at Shady Oaks hitting shag bags of balls. That gave Shady Oaks pro **Mike Wright** a ringside seat:*

I was real fortunate because I got to watch him hit a bunch of balls. Some pros have told me that about thirty years ago, when Hogan was playing in an event, guys would drop what they were doing and run over to the practice range, literally, to watch Hogan hit shots.

His practice routine here when he was in his seventies was to go out and practice for exercise. He did it almost every day for a long time. He would go out onto our little nine-hole course and kind of work his way through the bag. I would go out and just sit and watch him up close. It was pretty casual. Every now and then we would have small exchanges about shots or something. Then he would go pick up every ball with his shag bag.

He did not ever drive by and scoop a ball like we would do out of a cart. And he didn't have one of those tubes to poke them and pick them up. He would bend over and pick up each ball one by one and put it in his bag. And I asked him why, and he said he did it for exercise. Now you see pros—the least they are going to do is pop their ball up with their wedge and drop it in the shag bag, you know, something real casual. He was very definitive about picking up each ball one by one for exercise. It was kind of unique.

One of the most vivid memories for me was around 1987, when I was about twenty-seven and he was seventy-five. I had been the head pro for a short time, and I was out hitting balls in the morning on the little nine. For some reason he came out there and watched me hit some four-iron shots. I would have guessed I was hitting it 190 to 195 yards. Later that afternoon he was on the little nine hitting the ball with the same club exactly the same distance I was, and I wasn't a short hitter. And his clubs weren't even really built for distance. His shafts were stiff, but the grips were big and his clubfaces laid open. Anybody else hitting his clubs would have hit the ball high and right.

When most golfers go to the practice tee, they hit about fifteen to twenty balls with one club, then switch to another club, and so forth. Then there was the persevering Hogan's mode of practice, as recalled by **Gene Smyers:**

I'll tell you what his secret was: hard work and persistence. I'll tell you a story that I heard from Allen Baird,

Walking up and over hills took its toll on Hogan, meaning there was a big price to pay every time he played at Westchester, as he does here in 1970. (Jules Alexander photo)

chairman of Mrs. Baird's Bakery. He said as a kid about thirteen years old, he went over to Colonial one summer morning to play, and he saw Mr. Hogan practicing there. Allen said, "I went down there and asked if he minded if I just sat down and watched. He was hitting a four-wood. He hit that four-wood from about 9:30 until about 12:00, when he stopped, went over to the little snack bar, and got a Coke and a Hershey. He smoked a cigarette and sat down, and in about thirty minutes he went back out there and started hitting balls again. Where he had been hitting those balls from, there was no grass left. Still, he had used nothing but a four-wood the whole time. He hit that four-wood till about 3:30 or 4:00 in the afternoon."

I heard Ben say that he was the worst four-wood player on the tour. He said, "I determined I'd learned how to hit a four-wood. I reached the point where I could hit a four-wood closer than most pros could have hit a wedge. And I knew I could." He practiced and practiced and practiced. That's the secret of Hogan. He'd never had a pro teach him anything. I doubt that he ever asked another pro for any assistance. But the same thing was true of Byron Nelson, and was probably true with (Sam) Snead. And he made the comment about Snead: He said, "If I could have made the club selection and talked to Snead during a round, we'd all have played for second." He cited an example: Snead was leading the Masters coming into the last hole—I believe it was the last hole of the last round—and he said, "I drove by him maybe two yards and I didn't normally do that, but I did that time. We had a wind in our favor. I determined that I was going to hit either a five- or six-iron, and in all probability, a five. I knew if I hit a five, Sam, who usually hit a club longer than me, would hit a six. And I watched him. He took the four-iron out of his bag and I thought, 'He's going to choke this down,' but he flew the gallery."

———

Hogan was "sneaky long" when it came to hitting the golf ball. **Gene Smyers** *recalls just how surprising Hogan could be:*

One year John Schlee (then a PGA Tour player) came here—and this was before he had any success on the tour, and he had a terrible-looking set of golf clubs—and he sought Ben's help. Ben was patient and he offered to help John get a set of golf clubs. So that afternoon, the first afternoon he was here, Ben and Gary Laughlin and John and I played eighteen. Schlee was a tall, slender fellow, and he hit the ball quite a long way. Ben hit the ball to where he wanted the ball to be for the second shot. He also could hit it a long way, but he didn't do it very often. We got around to thirteen—Ben rode his own scooter, and Gary and I rode together, so John Schlee was in a scooter by himself. Everybody hit the ball off thirteen tee into the fairway, with Gary Laughlin and I both short of John and Ben. We took off down the fairway in our carts.

Ben never went to either of the shorter balls that were in the fairway. He pulled over to the side. And John Schlee went to the longest ball which was about twenty yards in front of the other ball. John pulled his cart off to the side, waiting for Ben to hit. And we were kind of at a stalemate, and Ben finally said, "John, it's your shot." Now, Ben had not looked at the ball, and neither had Schlee. How Ben knew that the ball wasn't his, I don't know. But I asked him about it later. And he said, "I knew I had hit the ball well. And I intended to hit it well. And I was trying to hit it a little longer than I normally do." He had outdriven Schlee by twenty yards, yet he had never looked at the ball. He just knew where it was. Schlee went out and looked at the balls and said, "Oh, sorry." And, of course, he was embarrassed.

Golf writer **Herbert Warren Wind,** *Hogan's coauthor on* Five Lessons, *had great insight into Hogan's golf game, as shown in the following excerpt from an article he wrote for the* New Yorker *preceding the 1955 U.S. Open at Olympic, where Hogan lost a playoff to Jack Fleck. Here, we pick up Wind writing in intricate detail about Hogan, in general, setting up for a shot:*

Other players go through the same motions, but they seldom give you the impression Hogan does—that he is genuinely thinking about what he is doing. Then, the mind made up, there is that light practice swing, the meticulous settling into his stance, the always-decisive stroke. If it has been a good shot, there is no expression on Hogan's part to show he acknowledges it as such. However, after he has played a poor shot at a stage of a tournament where it may be costly, there is a change of expression. The grin becomes ironic and his cold gray eyes widen and widen until they seem to be a full inch in height, and when you look at the man, so furious with himself, he is, as his colleagues refer to him, "the Hawk."[4]

<hr/>

Most amateur golfers concern themselves with what kind of golf balls they use to play a round, although Hogan would probably be more concerned with what kind of range balls he was playing with. After all, he hit many more range balls than he did balls for a nine- or eighteen-hole round. Shady Oaks pro **Mike Wright** *remembers just how particular Hogan could be when it came to range balls:*

One time we had gotten all new range balls. Mr. Hogan had stated that the range balls were tearing up the people's woods because they were too hard. He wasn't saying, "Oh boy, those dumb golf shop guys." He was just saying range balls in general. It had been my suggestion that we buy these range balls, so I was a little defensive.

At that time I was like, "Gosh, we just upgraded our range and we got all these new range balls, and Hogan is criticizing them." So I took some range balls and cut them in half and laid them on the counter. That way, if anybody commented about the range balls, I could say this is the same ball that you all are buying, which it was.

That was a childish kind of response on my part. Mr. Hogan heard that the new assistant pro had some balls on the counter, and I don't know if he said anything, but, anyway, he walked in one day and looked at the balls. He said, "What are these?" and I said, "Well, some of the members are complaining that the range balls are tearing up their clubs." I just wanted to show him that it was the same ball they were buying and playing with—very similar. He says, "That makes sense." And I never heard anybody complain about the range balls again.

Looking back on it, it was probably all a coincidence. I may have had a little bit of a defensive response to something that he had never even thought about.

Hogan, the Magnificent

I was scared of him, really. I heard he had a reputation for not wanting to get close to people.

—LEE TREVINO

Ben Hogan was full of surprises. There were times that he would pull shots out of his bag that amazed everyone, fans and fellow golfers alike, en route to winning another Masters or U.S. Open or hometown Colonial NIT or some such. But his golfing excellence was almost machinelike in its execution, so that whenever he did something unexpected with even a hint of flair, it was something to talk about.

Part of Hogan's color was a dry sense of humor that could come across as gruff, even curmudgeonly, to the untrained ear. He was also multifaceted. Although he spent thousands of hours banging buckets of balls and hobnobbing the lunch hour away with his cronies, Hogan found time to develop other talents, such as winning his share of fights in a boxing ring when he was a streetwise kid around Fort Worth or tapping into the

Hogan's grand plan to always hit fairways and greens sometimes went awry. This escape from the tree-lined rough took place in the 1950 Los Angeles Open, where he ultimately lost a playoff to Sam Snead in his comeback from a serious automobile mishap just eleven months earlier. (AP/Wide World Photos)

right side of his brain and creating artwork that merited gallery consideration.

Hogan was a magician, but instead of pulling a rabbit out of a hat, he would pull himself out of seclusion and suddenly be right there beside you before you knew what had hit you. Lee Trevino experienced that one time while playing a lights-out nine at Colonial. Years later, also at Colonial, Hogan protégé Kris Tschetter shot a record-setting 67 in the third round of the U.S. Open and found herself in an even bigger spotlight the next day while shooting a 75, because Hogan was in tow for a couple of holes.

There was more to Hogan than grouse and grind. He could surprise people by living and performing beyond their expectations on the golf course as well as off. Even well into his fifties, Hogan could outdrive the much-younger, muscle-rippled Arnold Palmer when the situation called for it, even if nothing was at stake but machismo. Also, Hogan used custom-built golf clubs that few of his peers could have broken 80 with. While in his eighties, Hogan—far removed from his everyday practice of hitting shag balls—one day dusted off his driver, and, acting either on impulse or spurred by an epiphany, went out, took three practice swings, and grouped three drives 250 yards away. He then walked out, picked up his balls, walked off the course, and disappeared back into hiding. Hogan was a Hollywood work of fiction, in life more fascinating than any movie on him could possibly be.

Hogan hitting a golf ball was the equivalent to anyone else riding a bike: Once you learn, you never forget how. One of the things that made Hogan such an amazing golfer, such an amazing man, was that in most respects he was at the top of his game even into his eighties. Despite being ravaged for the last fifty years of his life with leg and shoulder injuries sustained from the 1949 automobile accident, and despite having given up competitive golf for good at age fifty-eight in 1971, Hogan could still smack a golf ball with incredible power and accuracy until illnesses late in life finally took him off his feet. It got eerie at times, such as the day in the early 1990s when, out of the blue and having not touched a club in months, Hogan popped into the Shady Oaks pro shop en route to the locker room, where his golf clubs sat gathering dust. Shady Oaks head pro **Mike Wright** *picks it up from there:*

I will never forget the last balls I ever saw him hit. I think it was the last time in his life that he hit golf balls. And it just happened out of the blue. We had his clubs set in the back and they hadn't been touched for months. One day he walks into the golf shop, catching us off guard. He's got his golf shoes on and is wearing his sweater. I said, "Mr. Hogan, how can we help you?" He greeted us with something like "Hi, fellas," and then went back into the bag room. I didn't know what was going on and started to wonder if maybe he was just dusting his clubs or whatever. But then he comes back around the corner and he's got his driver in his hands. And he's got three balls.

He walks out the golf shop door, and I'm thinking, "What's going on here?" He goes up to the back of the tee on number 10, a par-four hole that plays about 370 yards into a south wind. The fairway opens up a little bit to the right, so if the pin were back left he would want to put it in the right side of the fairway. I'm just standing there in the shop, watching him. He puts a ball down on a tee, takes three practice swings with his wooden driver, and then hits it about 240 or 245 yards, a foot into the rough on the right side of the fairway, leaving him a perfect opening going back to the flag. I could tell he wasn't thrilled because of the way he wagged around a little bit. So he puts down the next ball and hits it about five yards farther and about two yards left of that first one, so that it's in the fairway—perfect position to hit to the green. He tees up another one and hits it within five feet of the second one.

No kidding, all these balls are grouped right together, out there about 245 or 250 yards. Now, I'm looking at this through binoculars. I can tell you that although the first ball was not perfect, it was slightly out of the fairway. The next two ended up something like five yards farther and three or four yards left—all were very close together. If you were playing the hole, his tee shots would have been ideal. I don't remember exactly what year this happened—he was in his eighties, but I had been around it so much that I took it for granted. I mean, it's not like he took a pitching wedge and hit it eighty yards or whatever to get a nice little grouping. We're talking a driver and hitting them out there 250 in a pile. Then he went out, picked up the balls, walked back in, and put his driver up. I never saw him hit another ball. I've always thought that maybe he just had a wild hair that he wanted to hit a driver and get the feel of it again. It was a slow day and there wasn't much going on. But it surprised me that he would do it right there on 10. He wasn't doing it to show off by any means. He just walked out there, picked them up, and came back in.

––––––––

Goofy golf was not something Hogan was particularly fond of, but there were those rare instances when he could be talked into taking a buddy's dare that was just too good to pass up, as long-time friend **Tex Moncrief** *discovered to his delight years ago:*

When we were members at Rivercrest—this was before Marvin Leonard opened Shady Oaks in 1958—we'd play a little golf, and every once in a while Ben would play with us. One day while we were talking and needling and all that, Hogan says to M. O. Rife Jr., a friend, "M. O., I could beat you standing on one leg with a two-iron." And M. O. said, "Well, I'll just bet you a thousand dollars that you can't." And Hogan said, "I'll take it." And I said, "Ben, I might take a couple thousand dollars of that myself." So I bet Ben a couple thousand dollars, and some other people made little bets either on him or M. O.

The next day Hogan played M. O. standing on his one leg—it didn't make any difference which one—with a two-iron; that's the only club he had. By the time we got around to the twelfth hole, ole M. O. had him dormie. Ben never finished the twelfth hole. He just took his clubs and left, conceding the match, although he didn't say he was conceding. He didn't say a dang thing. He just left. He was in the clubhouse later after we all came in, and he was kind of cussing himself and saying a few things to us. He said, "You know, I spend all my life trying to be a good golfer and then come out and get some handicap or some silly bet like that. I'm never going to play with you again." Prostituting his golf game—he didn't like that very much, goofing around like that. I guess if he never actually verbally conceded, he can say that he never lost the golf match.

———

When it came to golf being played as it should be, Hogan always seemed to have another level to where he could take his game. All one had to do was ask, under the right circumstances, as fellow Texan and longtime touring pro **Rocky Thompson** *learned to his amazement one time:*

I saw him give an exhibition in Abilene, Texas, and this is bizarre. It's the only day in the history of Abilene that there wasn't a breath of wind—in the history of the city. God knew that Mr.-Ben-Hogan-the-greatest-ballstriker-who-has-ever-lived was going to give an exhibition that day. There were about four hundred people out there at Abilene Country Club that day, and I was sitting right behind him. He hit every shot perfect, except one. He hit a fat five-iron with his club hitting the ground about six inches behind the ball. Then he continues on to hit ten perfect five-irons. This sounds impossible—he would hit those five-irons and they would draw about two yards at their peak and then would fall to the right about five yards. His driver would actually draw—and I had perfect vision, I was fifteen years old—and that ball would take off with a two-yard draw and get right to that peak and then would fall down to the right. That caddie was sitting out there with a shag bag, and that ball would land and with one hop he'd catch it in a towel and then put it in the bag. Then he'd step a foot this way, catch it in the towel, and put it in the bag. Then he'd step this way, catch it in the towel, and put it in the bag.

Finally, this lunkhead—after Hogan had hit about four perfect tee shots—said, "Ben, why don't you *really* hit one." And I thought he had just hit four perfect drives about as good as he could possibly hit it. He said, "Okay," and I'm thinking, "Oh, jeez, he's got another gear!" And he takes his right foot and sticks it about five inches farther back behind him. Then he rocked back on that thing, and that ball took off hooking just like the others, and it fell to the right and that ball hit about eighteen to twenty yards past where the others had hit—

and with the exact same flight. He was the *greatest-ball-striker-who-has-ever-lived!*

—⚞⚟—

Max, one of the dogs Hogan befriended at Shady Oaks, actually became one of Hogan's favorite practice companions, as **Tim Scott** *of Fort Worth points out. Scott worked for Hogan as a marketing executive at the Hogan Company for thirteen years (1969–81) and offers this story of Ben and Max, excerpted from a book Scott is writing about Hogan:*

One of the humorous, ongoing sagas around Shady Oaks Country Club in the late seventies and early eighties was the story of Max, the infamous Max, a black and white mutt that looked like a large Border collie but might have been part shepherd. Max became a legend around Shady Oaks because of his affinity for watching Hogan hit practice balls. When Hogan got into his golf cart to go hit practice balls, Max would climb aboard the cart and go along. Max would get right up on the passenger seat next to Hogan with head up and body erect, almost like he was at "attention," and ride out onto the golf course, just as if he were the caddie going out with Hogan to retrieve Hogan's golf balls. Upon arrival at the designated practice spot—a spot Hogan would choose where the wind or breeze was blowing from his right to left— Max would climb down, lie beside the golf cart with his head between his front paws, and patiently watch Hogan hit his practice balls.

When practice was over, Max would climb back up onto the seat of the cart and ride back to the clubhouse with Hogan. It was uncanny—Max wouldn't watch

Decades before he was giving exhibitions and winning majors, Hogan was just another young hopeful trying to piece together a game good enough to handle the rigors of the pro golf tour back in the thirties. This shows him at age twenty-two in a photo he signed for his brother and sister-in-law, Royal and Margaret Hogan. (Photograph provided courtesy of Jacqueline Hogan Towery)

anyone else hit balls, just Ben Hogan. That dog probably saw more Hogan swings than any one person, and it probably spoiled him because of his apparent disinterest toward all other golfers.

One year Hogan decided to go to Florida to practice and play at Seminole Golf Club near Palm Beach. Gary Laughlin, one of Hogan's golfing buddies, decided to play a practical joke on Hogan. Gary typed up a letter from Max telling Hogan how lonely and mistreated he felt because Hogan was away from Shady Oaks and in far-away Florida. "Max" said he missed Ben and wasn't eating right, and the members weren't taking care of him like Ben did. Gary then inked Max's paw print at the bottom of the letter and mailed it to Hogan at Seminole.

Hogan got such a kick out of it that he carried the letter with him to show everyone during his Florida stay. Gary even claimed that Hogan took it with him to a black-tie event and showed the letter to everyone he met at the party.

In 1980 a sportswriter for the *Dallas Morning News* wrote a column about Hogan and included a comment about Max, "the club dog" sitting "obediently while Hogan strikes ball after ball after ball." In response, Hogan wrote the columnist a letter complimenting him on the column about Max, but in the letter Hogan also cautioned:

"There is a problem, however, stemming from your article in that Max is suing me for contributory negligence. You recall that you called Max 'the club dog.' Everyone, including Max, knows he is not a dog, but that he is President, Chairman of the Board, and protector of the club's membership.

"I have explained to Max that this article was written unbeknown to me, but he will not accept that. Our relationship is rather strained in that when I speak to him now he wags his tail very slightly, whereas in the past he would give me a vigorous waggle. Also, he has stopped watching me practice. This, of course, really puts me down since he was my last gallerite (sic).

"I will try to settle this suit out of court for a few quarter pounders, but if Max refuses and requests a jury trial, I am positive I will lose this case and he will be awarded the whole herd of Santa Gertrudis from the King Ranch."

Ben Hogan had a great sense of humor, and he enjoyed a good laugh. His letter to the sportswriter is a good example of some of the humor Hogan would display from time to time.

Wherever he went, Hogan drew a crowd, not only because of his glorious past and fame, but also because his public appearances were so few and far between. One of those rare occasions that drew instant notoriety occurred at Colonial Country Club in July 1991, during the U.S. Women's Open. Hogan protégé **Kris Tschetter,** *a TCU alum and, at the time, a Fort Worth resident, inspired an impromptu appearance by Hogan the day after she had shot a then women's tournament course record 67 to vault into Open leader-board contention. Tschetter chuckles at the memory:*

I knew the Open was going to be there and I kept saying to him, "Are you going to come out—are you going to be there?" He would say, "Oh, yeah, yeah, I'll be there." But

I knew he wouldn't, because he absolutely doesn't like going out in public. Even though he kept saying he would be there, I really doubted he would be.

After I would play each day at Colonial that week, I'd go out to Shady Oaks and tell him what was going on. On Sunday I had a chance to win, but didn't play very well and shot something like a 75. Mr. Hogan and his wife were watching it on TV and—as Valerie told me years later—he wasn't going to go because he felt like the spotlight would get taken away from me if I had a good day. But when it turned out I wasn't playing well, he decided he needed to be there for me. That's pretty neat. They came out and he showed up at the sixteenth hole, watched me tee off on seventeen, and then went over to eighteen to watch me come in. I was just excited that he would come out. In fact, I was really surprised because I didn't expect him to be there. I just remember being happy that he would bite the bullet and come out there. And he goes, "Oh, I wouldn't have missed it for the world." Valerie told me later that he would rather be there for me on a bad day than on a good day.

At that point, no one really knew that I knew him except for some close friends. I had never really told anyone about it. But at each tournament after the '91 Open, that's what people wanted to talk to me about. My respect for him is why I never really told anyone. He wanted people to like him because he was a nice person, not because he was a good golfer. It's weird, because when I think about him, I think about him as my friend. Then I'll step back from that and think, "Wow, I was able to do something that a lot of people would have given their right arm for—to watch him hit balls and to play nine holes with him." I was very lucky.

John Jacobs, tour veteran and younger brother to Hogan pal Tommy Jacobs, never saw a lot of Hogan, but he saw enough to know firsthand just how intriguing and mysterious Hogan could be:

I was in the army at Fort Hood, Texas, in 1964 when I went up to Fort Worth to watch my brother Tommy play in the Colonial. Hogan was up there hitting balls, and I joined him for about three holes over at Shady Oaks. He never said a word to me. I hit the ball terribly and I expected him to say something, but he never said anything except, "Tell your brother hello and I'll see you later." I watched him practice for about an hour and a half, and the caddie was looking into the sun and was ducking every other shot. Hogan was hitting between three- and five-irons, and his caddie couldn't see them to catch them, and he was ducking because Hogan was almost hitting him with every shot.

I don't think Hogan played Colonial that year. The other time I saw him play, I saw him play at Cherry Hills in 1960 at the U.S. Open. I went off to watch (Jack) Nicklaus, because when you're fifteen years old, anybody in his forties looks like they're a hundred. Nicklaus was the guy to watch, but I saw Hogan hit every green for like thirty-four holes. It didn't take me long to figure out this guy played tee to green better than anyone else did.

For many years, fellow golfing great **Lee Trevino** *lived less than an hour's drive away from Hogan's home and Shady Oaks hangout, although he never was afforded the opportunity to spend ample time with Hogan. But on one special occasion for Trevino, Hogan was behind him all the way, without Merry Mex's even knowing about it:*

When it came to golf in Texas, we believed he could part the Red Sea. I was scared of him, really. I heard he had a reputation for not wanting to get close to people. I guess maybe I respected him for his privacy too much. With his living in Fort Worth and my living in Dallas, I probably had lots of times and chances where I could have gone and tried to see him.

I remember one time, I think it was in 1977, that I was playing Colonial, and I hit the flag at eighteen with a six-iron and then made the putt for a birdie. That gave me a back-nine 29, and I later found out that he had been following me part of the time in a golf cart. I had no idea that he had been out there.

There was no predicting who Hogan would next choose to befriend, and the recipient of Hogan's attention usually was the most surprised of all. Such was the case with **Al Geiberger,** *a relative unknown very early in his PGA Tour career when he first met Hogan—with Hogan initiating the introduction, no less:*

I didn't really know Ben Hogan very well, but my story was that he knew me. He was sitting out there at Colonial one day, and I came walking by. I figured he wouldn't even pay attention to me or even know who I was. And he said, "Hey, Al, you've been playing really well, and I really like your game." I didn't even know Ben Hogan knew I existed. This was back in the early sixties, probably the first time I played Colonial. I have no idea what I had done that had gotten his attention. But that goes to show he was aware of a lot more things than anyone might have thought. He was taking in what was going on with other players and what was happening, even if it didn't look that way.

---

*Count **George Archer** among those few pro golfers not from Hogan's generation who gained Hogan's respect without even trying, and this was after thinking (erroneously) that he had gotten off to a rocky start in their relationship. At one point, Archer thought Hogan—Hogan!!—was attempting to psych him out on the golf course by talking him to death:*

The first time I met Ben Hogan officially, I was paired with him on Sunday in my first Masters. He had shot a very good back nine on Saturday and both of us were two off the lead, I think. The night before we played, I said to myself, "Well, when I'm an old man, I'm going to remember that I played with Ben Hogan and that's going to be something. So although I'm going to be too nervous to play well, I'm going to enjoy the day."

I go out there the next day and can remember going up to him on the first hole and saying, "Mr. Hogan, George Archer." He just nodded his head, and I shook his hand. He teed off and hit a good drive, and then I went up there and drove it in the fairway. By this time, he was standing on the end of the tee up ahead. When I picked up my tee, I could see him standing there looking back at me and I was thinking, "Jeez, I didn't do anything wrong. I mean, I didn't move when he hit or anything like that, so what in the hell is he going to start chewing me out now for." I mean I was pretty intimidated.

So I got up next to him and he said, "George, that was very nice playing last week." I had won the week before in Greensboro, and now he starts talking, and we walk down the hill and he's talking, and he's talking and we walk to the bottom of the hill, and he's still talking, and we walk all the way up to the sand trap, and he's talking the whole time. My head is spinning around and I'm thinking, "What in the hell is going on here? The ice man, what is he doing? *Oh! I get it: He's going to talk me to death, I see.*" All of a sudden I broke out laughing and he looked up at me and I said, "Excuse me, Mr. Hogan, I'm away," and I went over to my ball to hit. And I'm laughing because I was thinking, "Who the hell am I to think that Mr. Hogan is going to reverse-psychology me and talk me to death."

Everything I had heard all my life—like he never says a word and you might get a "You're away" once in a while, and he never says nice shot or anything like that—that was not the Ben Hogan I played with. He was very cordial that day. We talked quite a few times while sitting on benches that day. The whole time I'm thinking, "Is this the Ben Hogan I've read and heard about?" He didn't play well—he hit about three bad shots, and he paid dearly for them. I got a two-stroke penalty and shot like a 78 and think he shot a 75, and we both finished well back.

I played with him again the next year and with Arnold Palmer. That was an interesting day because twenty thousand people were out there watching Palmer and Hogan, and I was in the way. I'll never forget the third hole, where Palmer hit one of those low drives and the crowd roared like crazy. Hogan took the cigarette out of his mouth and threw it down on the ground. He threw it so hard, it bounced off my shoe. I was stunned. He then hit this little low fade and people clapped because it was down the middle. I then hit a three-wood down the left side. When we got down there, there was one ball about even with me and then the third ball about eighty yards ahead.

I got down there first to my ball. Meanwhile, Hogan and Palmer were walking and talking, and their caddies were with them, and all four walked right by the first ball near me, and they all went to the long ball up ahead. So I'm thinking, "Who's going to be the one to have to turn around and walk back to his?" Hogan got down there and never looked at the ball. He just puffed on his cigarette and looked at the green. Palmer had to bend over and look at the ball, and then turn around and walk back to his ball. And the crowd was like, "Woooooooooo." Hogan sent a message there that was unreal, and that was, "There would be no more screaming for those Arnold Palmer drives." And there wasn't. He had a sand wedge to the green and the hole was about 400 yards long, so he had hit his drive about 310. Hogan was long when he wanted to be long. He could really rip it.

———

*After about the age of forty-five, Hogan's putting went straight downhill, and that included uphill and sidehill putts as well as flat and downhill ones. He didn't just have the yips; he had the shakes, and was at times unable even to take the putter back. Tee to green, however, he still had few peers. Even with his hands shaking, however, Hogan would occasionally put together the superlative round, as **Bob Charles** witnessed in the early 1960s:*

When I was sixteen or seventeen years of age, I bought his book *Power Golf*. I don't think I ever read it—I just looked at the pictures. Later I played with him on four or five occasions. One round I played with him was in the Carling World Open at Oakland Hills in Detroit, and I think it was in the last round. He shot 67 and hit every fairway and every green. The thing I remembered most was that his hands were shaking. He couldn't keep the putter still because his hands were shaking so much, and yet he never missed a putt of under ten feet. I think that was the most amazing exhibition of putting I have ever seen. No one has ever perfected the game of golf, but in my book he was the closest that anyone ever came. He had more ball control than anybody I've ever seen in the game.

—◆—

*If Hogan could have maintained even an average putting stroke, it's conceivable that he could have won a major title or two while in his fifties. The U.S. Open wasn't the only 1960 major in which Hogan, then in his late forties, played well enough to win, as **Lionel Hebert** attests:*

Hogan takes dead aim at the 1959 U.S. Open at Winged Foot. (Jules Alexander photo)

I played with Hogan in the 1960 PGA Championship at Akron. I couldn't believe how long that course was. I played one practice round where I was able to hit only two irons in nine holes. I ended up playing thirty-six holes of the tournament with Hogan and Ted Kroll, and I can still remember Hogan hitting every green but one in that stretch. The one he missed was the seventh green, a par-three, where he hit his tee shot into a bunker on the right. He then knocked it to about three inches for the tap-in par, and that turned out to be the only one-putt green he had the entire two days. That's when I thought he was going to quit playing. He could really strike the ball well, but there were times that he would leave putts ten to twelve feet short of the hole.

Tommy Jacobs once took the surreptitious route in trying to gather some intelligence about Hogan's game, starting with his golf clubs:

One time I sneaked into the bag room at Colonial Country Club, got every club out of his golf bag and checked the swing weights and shaft lengths on each of them. He played True Temper shafts and had MDI flex in his irons and MDW in his woods. I then ordered a set of clubs with the exact same specs through Wilson, which I was with at the time. When I got the order back, I took the clubs out and started hitting with them, and the shafts were so stiff that I couldn't get any feel for them. It was like trying to swing a two-by-four. My mouth dropped.

Most golfers dream of getting a hole in one every time they step onto the tee of a par-three hole. Not Hogan. As roundtable companion Gene Smyers points out, Hogan never purposely shot for the pin on the short holes:

One time we got on the subject of how many holes in one he had made. "Well," he said, "I never did try to make holes in one. That wasn't my goal because when I shot for the pin, I *hit* the pins. That was when they had the wooden pins. When you did that, the ball might bounce off thirty or forty yards, and I wouldn't have a birdie. I wouldn't even have a par. It might bounce to where I'd have a tough recovery shot."

In conjunction with that, he told a story about playing early on in his career, when he wasn't able to make it—he didn't have the backing financially—and was playing in either Tucson or Phoenix, and they had the wooden pins. He said those wooden pins had steel fittings that the wood was set in, and the wood would swell when it got wet, such as when they watered the course or it rained. At one point "the caddie was holding the pin," he said, "and I putted—it was a rather long putt—and the pin wouldn't come out. It was stuck, and when my ball hit the pin it was a two-stroke penalty. That kept me from winning the tournament, and I was not able to stay on the tour because I didn't have enough money to continue. I had to come back to Fort Worth. That's why my objective early on was to avoid hitting the pin, because that would not enable me to have a birdie putt."

———

*Hogan didn't just know golf; he knew the golf swing, and he drew on comparisons to a proper batting swing in baseball to point out something to his friend **Bob Wynne**. To this day Wynne believes he might have been the unwitting recipient of Hogan's so-called secret:*

In the early eighties my son Mitch and I were getting ready to tee off at number ten and here comes Hogan. I'm thinking, "Uh-oh, he's coming over to get on me about something." Instead, he just reaches into Mitch's bag, pulls out a three-iron, looks at Mitch, looks at me, and then he says, "You all know who Ted Williams was?" And I said, "Yes sir, in my opinion, he was the best hitter of a baseball there ever was."

"Well," he said, "I had the pleasure of meeting him one time, and let me show you something." He took that three-iron and took a stance like a baseball player at the plate. And he said, "Now let me show you how he swung." Now Williams was a left-hander, but Hogan's swing was just like Ted Williams's, and you get the feeling that he could have been good at hitting the baseball. With each swing, he started going down six inches at a time, repeating the same swing all the way down to ground level while saying to us, "Do you see what I'm doing?" Then he said, "You swing a golf club the same way you swing a bat in baseball."

I never forgot that. I knew better than to grill him about that because he probably would have walked away. He expected you to understand, then go do it.

Shortly before he died, I asked him if he had a secret. His response was, "I've shown you." He didn't say, "I told you." A few months ago (1999) I was watching the Golf Channel on television one night when Sam Snead was being interviewed. Sam was asked if he thought Hogan had a secret. His response was that he had probably played more rounds with Hogan than anyone, and the most unusual thing about his swing was the way he finished the follow-through with his right arm straight. That statement brought back memories of the Ted Williams episode. Was this his secret?

———

A round of golf was a rare feat for Hogan after about 1985, although he continued to practice diligently up until he was too sick in the last few years leading up to his death in 1997. As LPGA tour golfer-to-be **Kris Tschetter** *found out during her playing days at TCU—which often included sojourns over to Shady Oaks—Hogan always had an amazing shot up his sleeve:*

I played nine holes with him one time, although there were other times we'd play a few holes. The one round I played with him was with two other girls on the TCU team at the time—Kirsten Larson and Ellie Gibson. He shot even par from the back tees—this was probably in '87. He wasn't hitting it real far and he could hardly see—we were having to tell him where the pin was. I especially remember a shot he hit on the first hole (a par-four). He hit his second shot over the green, then pulled out a pitching wedge. We thought he sculled it—he hit this low thing and it's going hard. It takes one hop and stops about a foot from the hole. We just looked at each other like, "Did we just see that?" He was just amazing.

It was considered an honor to shag balls for Hogan on the practice range, although it could be scary at times, too. Hogan typically would have the boy stand out in a designated landing area and then use the boy as his target. For Hogan, it was business as usual; for the caddie, it should have been hard-hat time, as **Gene Smyers** *recalls:*

I remember one afternoon when a group of us were watching him hit balls. There was a kid that was shagging balls for him for the first time. I think he was a high school kid. Ben was in his usual spot by the eighteenth tee and he hit two or three balls, and this kid was moving around down there shagging for him. Ben was hitting a long iron and motioned for the kid to come back to him, and said, "Son, stand still, you're my target. I can't hit a moving target." The kid said, "But Mr. Hogan, that's why I'm not standing still. You almost hit me every time." And Hogan said, "Well, you watch when I hit and you follow the ball. It won't hit you. You step out of the way." Soon the shag boy could almost pick the balls up on the first bounce. Hogan was that accurate. But this young fellow was scared to death. When he went back out there, it occurred to me that he really needed to be wearing some head gear.

———

Another amazing thing about Hogan was his capacity to surprise people in social situations by making it a point to know who they were before they had been formally introduced. **Ken Venturi** *remembers just such a scenario, when he took his new bride, Beau, to meet Ben and Valerie for the first time at a club in New York City:*

He had a great humor. He couldn't turn on and off the switch. He never went to big parties or dinners. But he would go out a lot and he would go out with (Cary) Middlecoff a lot. He never socialized with Sam (Snead) at all. It would be just a very few to dinner.

After I got married to Beau, I didn't know that Ben knew who Beau was. There was no reason for him to know her because they'd never met. So we were at 21 in New York one night just after we were married, and we're at the round bar getting ready to get seated. I look around in the room, that circular room at the bar where they eat, and there was Ben and Valerie. And Beau says to me, "Oh, my gosh, there's Ben Hogan." And I said, "Well, I'll be darned." So I took her hand and said, "Come on over."

I get within about ten feet of the table and Ben stands up and says, "Beau; Hennie Bogan." That's what he used to call himself at times—Hennie Bogan. He said, "I knew Ken would finally get smart and marry himself a good Fort Worth girl, and what a pleasure it is to see you and to meet you. I've heard so much about you." *She nearly passed out.* He knew all about her, and I had no idea that he even knew what was going on. And Valerie got up and she gave me a kiss.

———

Even "the King," **Arnold Palmer,** *was in awe of Hogan at one time—and who's to say he still isn't, deep down?*

I'd seen Ben Hogan at various tournaments and even played in a group close to him at Wilmington, but I met him for the first time in Augusta. To be honest, I was so in awe of the man, and so naturally shy, I felt he was utterly unapproachable. At the Masters someone introduced us, and we shook hands. He was polite enough, but I felt the cool distance others sensed while in his presence. Hogan was still limping from his (1949) car crash but remained the most dangerous player of his age, maybe the best ballstriker who ever lived. I was at first surprised by—and later angered about—the fact that he never, in the years I knew him, called me by my first name. Ten million golf fans have felt completely comfortable calling me "Arnie," but Mr. Hogan never spoke my real name. He only called me "fella." To give him the benefit of the doubt, he called lots of young, ambitious players "fella." Perhaps he couldn't remember their names (after all, a lot of talent was streaming out of the college ranks into the professional ranks), or maybe he sensed that others and I were gunning for his records, which of course we were. But he was a living legend and inspiration.[5]

Hogan's memory, at least when it came to golf tournaments and golf courses, at times bordered on spooky. **Bob Wynne** *remembers one occasion in Hogan's twilight years when the Hawk amazed everyone present by his uncanny recall of the layout of a course he probably hadn't played in more than twenty years:*

A friend of mine called me one day and asked if I could get Hogan to sign the scorecard used in the *Shell's Wonderful World of Golf* match between him and Snead played at the Houston Country Club. The building there had since burned, along with the signed card. They already had Sam's signature on the new card and needed Hogan's. I invited the guy to come have lunch with me at Shady Oaks and there I'd get the signature for him. When Mr. Hogan was presented the card, he looked at it and handed it back to me. He said, "Bob, I didn't play this course," and he named a hole, maybe two, where the par was wrong, and he proceeded to tell us exactly what he and Snead had scored on each hole. The Houston member was incredulous and told us that those holes had been changed and Hogan was exactly right. Mr. Hogan signed the card.

Byron Nelson *will forever be linked in golf history with his crosstown rival Hogan, and he recalls Hogan as a tough scrapper in two arenas, not just golf:*

That Christmas (apparently 1926, at Fort Worth's Glen Garden Country Club) they had the caddie championship again, but this time it was just nine holes, not eighteen. By sinking a long putt on the last hole, I tied with a small, dark-complected boy named Ben Hogan. Par was 37, and we both shot 40. The members decided since it wasn't dark and the weather was good, we would go another nine holes . . . I was fortunate and won by one shot, so that was the first time I played against Ben and beat him . . . They gave us each a golf club—mine was a five-iron and he got a two-iron. Well, I already had a five, and he already had a two, so we traded clubs.

I had met Ben before, of course, but hadn't really gotten to know him. He lived across town and went to a different school, and I didn't see him except at Glen Garden. Though he was short, he had big hands and arms for his size. He was quiet, serious, and mostly kept to himself. The first time I was really aware of him was Christmas the year before, when the members put on a little boxing match for entertainment. Ben liked to box, and so did another caddie we called Joe Boy. They boxed for about fifteen minutes, I guess, but nobody got knocked down or hurt. I was just watching, because I never did like to box or fight. When the members decided it was over, they all gave Ben and Joe Boy a big hand.[6]

Just how precious was it to be in Hogan's presence, sharing insightful conversation with him? Precious enough for **George Archer** *to one day let playing partner Julius Boros, himself a* *past U.S. Open champion, to continue playing on by himself while he (Archer) stopped at the turn at Shady Oaks to chat with Hogan:*

Ben saw me and came out of the clubhouse to talk to me for about a half an hour. Boros just went off and left me, and so I played 10 and 11 by himself. I figured I had a choice: I could go off and keep playing with Boros or I could talk to Hogan. I decided to talk to Hogan. I must have done something he liked, whether it was the way I played or the way I conducted myself. I think he liked me. I could just tell that. It was a warm afternoon, and he asked me about my golf and something about a surgery I had had—he just knew about me. But I never asked him for any advice. When I was young, I had paid for a lesson from Bud Ward, who was a friend of Hogan's, and like Hogan he was a short man. However, I don't think short men should tell tall men how to play golf. So I never asked Hogan for any advice because I could never emulate what he did with his swing.

Okay, so we know that Hogan could golf and that at one time he could box. **George Archer** *saw another side of Hogan's creative genius one year while sitting with Hogan at a Masters Champions Dinner:*

He came to the Masters Champions Dinner the year after I won the Masters (in 1969). As defending champion, I got to do the seating arrangement and put Mr. Hogan right beside me. And I found out that night that Ben Hogan was a very good artist. He could draw horses with wings, dinosaurs—all kinds of mythical characters. He took a pen and he drew about four animals. I'm looking at this and I'm thinking, "God, if I had any nerve at all, I would get these things framed and have him sign them." But I was chicken. I didn't say anything and they just went in the laundry. Such detail, too. I sure wish I had taken them. I wish I had told the waiter, "I'll give you twenty bucks or whatever for those tablecloths," but being young I didn't want to do something that was wrong at the Masters.

Charlie Hudson, head waiter at Shady Oaks for more than forty years, was a dutiful attendant working Hogan's table for several decades, and Hogan once surprised him with an unexpected act of generosity:

One time we went shopping. This was after he had gone to the clothing store to get fitted for some suits, sport coats and pants. He went up there but got lost. He made it back to the club and got back to the table and sat down. I didn't know a thing about it, of course. But his wife called me and said, "Charles, Mr. Hogan was supposed to go to get fitted for some suits and apparently he didn't make it. Will you take him up there?" I said I sure would. So I went to Mr. Hogan and said, "Let's go get the new suits." He goes, "Okay then."

So I take him up there to get him fitted. I was sitting down and waiting on him. He kept looking for me to make sure I was there with him. I said, "I'm right here." All he had to do was get fitted for the suits, so then we're ready to go. We started to go, but then he told the salesman to fit me, too. I said no. He said to the salesman, "I said to fit him, too." And I said, "Okay." So I got a suit—an Oxford; brown double-breasted. He stayed there and

Hogan could generate a lot of power when he needed it, driving his legs into and through the ball. (Jules Alexander photo)

watched me get fitted. Besides, I was driving the car and he had to wait for me.

———

Gary McCord, a CBS-TV golf analyst and Senior PGA Tour golfer, has one Hogan story that assured him that Hogan played golf only to win:

I went over to meet Hogan with Frank Chirkinian and Ken Venturi, and I went over there to sit with him at Shady Oaks. It was just the three of us with him. He kept looking at me and he finally said, "What do you do?" I didn't say anything, and Frank goes, "He's an announcer, for us." And Ken goes, "He also played the tour."

When Hogan would talk to you, he'd ask you a question, then go back and talk to the other guys. He said, "How long you been on the tour?" I said, "Fifteen years." Then he turned around and started talking to Frank. Then he turned back around to me and asked, "How many did you win?" Before I could answer, he turned around and started talking to Frank, and I said, "Well, none." A minute later, he again turned around and said, "Why are you still playing?" I said, "That's a very good question."

———

Even when Hogan wasn't present in body, his influence was powerful, even when communicated through photos, as PGA Tour veteran Joel Edwards experienced at thirty-five thousand feet one stormy day:

A guy about sixty years old walked up to me—he was in first class, I was in coach. He said, "If anyone on this airplane could appreciate these . . ." It was a two-and-a-half-hour flight. He handed me a big, thick envelope and there were probably five hundred pictures in there of Ben Hogan swinging a golf club. This guy was one of Mr. Hogan's really good friends, a Mr. Gibson. He said, "Mr. Hogan let me take a bunch of pictures of him over the years, and I figured I'd let you see them." I sat there the whole flight—it was a terrible flight, lots of turbulence, the plane bouncing all over the place—but I really don't remember being at all bothered by it because I was staring at these pictures, all black and white, the whole time.

Anyone who saw the demolished Cadillac in which Ben and Valerie had almost been killed in 1949 went away believing it had to be something close to a miracle that either survived.
Marty Leonard, *the daughter of Hogan mentor and benefactor Marvin Leonard, never has been able to shake the image that she saw when she was a teenager:*

One of the vivid memories that I have, and it's never a very pleasant one, was the accident. I remember Daddy getting a phone call in the middle of the night and then helping arrange through his air force contacts to get the doctors out to Van Horn to do the surgery. Later, the wrecked automobile was brought back to Fort Worth and displayed as a safety council thing—they were trying to promote safety. I remember going down and seeing it with a big sign saying that this was the accident that Ben Hogan was in. It was just obvious from the way the steering wheel had gone through the driver's seat that he would not have survived if he had been in that seat. He literally jumped over onto Valerie in the passenger seat. Whether that was a natural reaction or he was consciously trying to protect her, I don't know.

—⸺⟊⟊⸺—

Veteran television sports commentator **Jack Whitaker** *wrote that one of his favorite stories about Hogan concerns a story that Hogan told him involving a dangerous airplane flight:*

One year at the Colonial Invitational in Fort Worth, a tournament Hogan had won five times, I was the guest speaker at the dinner they hold for former champions. To my great delight, they seated me on the dais between Valerie Hogan and Ben, and the Hawk was in a talkative mood.

"Is there anything you'd like to know about any of those old golfers?" he asked me. "I've had a lot of great times with them."

"See that fellow," he said, pointing to Johnny Bulla. "Right after the war, he had gotten ahold of a second-hand airplane. We were playing in Florida, and about ten of us decided to chip in and fly to our next tournament, which was in Arizona. I was the copilot. When we got to Arizona, I had to make an emergency landing, and I damn near crashed the plane. It would have wiped out half the golf tour. That was the end of Golf Tour Airlines."[7]

HOGAN, THE MENTOR

I can't pinpoint where I learned what I learned. It almost seems kind of ingrained now, and that's from spending time with him.

—KRIS TSCHETTER

An old baseball maxim says that the greatest players make the worst managers, although that theory doesn't cut it in golf. Good golfers with unorthodox swings know enough of the swing basics to help any amateur golfer, and Hogan really wasn't an unorthodox golfer. Experts say that Hogan's swing was classic, a claim influenced no doubt by the existence of Hogan's enormously popular instructional *Five Lessons*. But compared to the modern, powerful, and silky swings of today's golfers such as Fred Couples and Ernie Els, Hogan's slashing swing is more Ernie Banks than Ernie Els. Hogan's swing plane was relatively flat and he slashed hard at the ball, but he knew enough about what he was doing, thinking, and visualizing to possess a wealth of information worth its weight in gold when passed along. Years of digging his impeccable game out of the dirt had taught him well.

Hogan, however, didn't really pass along much of what he knew of the swing, or did he? Anyone who knows the difference between a wedge and a wedgie has by now heard about Hogan's so-called secret, the one swing key that could supposedly turn a good PGA Tour pro into the winningest golfer of all time. In his own reclusive, tightlipped way, Hogan taunted the world by holding his alleged Secret close to his vest. Theorists and swing doctors the world over have taken stabs at guessing what it was, with most such hypotheses centering around the position of the wrists, hands, and/or arms at takeaway and at impact.

Whether or not there ever really was a Secret doesn't matter. Life would be back to boring in golf if the Secret wasn't up there with the grassy knoll and Bubba's "love" life in continual debates. Hogan didn't work seriously with many golfers. For those that he did work with, he was the whole package, perhaps even better than a double dose of David Leadbetter and Butch Harmon. Hogan tweaked swings and offered revelatory tips here and there, but most of what he expounded on were the intangibles, such as course management and clearing one's mind to play foolproof tournament golf. Spend enough time with Hogan, and what he had to offer would rub off, even if it was just an isolated dose of inspiration.

Two of Hogan's long-term "apprentices" of recent years were a pair of current thirty-somethings—Kris Tschetter, an LPGA tour veteran, and Tom Byrum, a PGA Tour counterpart. Both chip in with their remembrances of Hogan, the mentor, in this chapter, and what they commonly share is a belief that the most valuable lessons taught by Hogan didn't involve specific swing keys. It was more a process of osmosis, with Hogan touching on all facets of the game, mental and physical, and letting them reshape their own games by assimilating his general guidelines. Then again, there is a hint that Hogan told them of things he wanted them to forever keep to themselves. So the rest of us—we, the great neglected—can only suspect that Tschetter, Byrum, and a few other golfers similarly blessed by Hogan's counsel of years past carry his little Secrets around with them.

Ben Hogan went to his deathbed in 1997 apparently still in sole possession of the so-called Secret to the golf swing, the key that would supposedly unlock the mystery to shooting great score after great score. It is generally assumed that Hogan gave away bits and pieces of his swing secrets to golfers he mentored over the years, but like pieces of a jigsaw puzzle, no one has ever put them all together into one conclusive swing solution. CBS-TV golf analyst **Ken Venturi,** *a close friend of Hogan's and a recipient of much of Hogan's golf wisdom, weighs in with what he thought Hogan's secret was:*

It was Hogan. That was the secret. He had one secret. He said, "Muscles do not have memories. I tell my muscles what to do." He could visualize everything that he was doing in his golf swing. If you'll look at the *Hogan Mystique* book, you can see the multitude of different swings in there. He could create that image in his mind of what he wanted to do to make the swing do what he has to do—whether it be a low draw, high draw, a high fade, a knockdown, a feather shot. He's got all these finishes and all these swings that he created himself to create the shot that he had visualized in his mind. Now, he had some other things about his grip and his takeaway and elbows and things like that. He told me and Chirkinian one time, "It's the secret of elbow to elbow, where when you take it back, your right elbow is down and when you go through, your left elbow is down." That is basically where Hogan was at.

Hogan was not a teacher. Byron Nelson could teach: He could volunteer it. With Hogan, you had to ask him: "What do you feel like when you are doing this?" "What do you have in your mind when you're going to play this shot?" He would say, "Well, I'd do this . . ." and he could never say, "Ken, you ought to be doing this, this, and this." You had to pick his brain, and not many people could get into his brain because he wouldn't tell you. And so he would say, "This is what you do." If you played with Hogan and the pin was on the right-hand side next to a creek, and you swooped it over the creek and knocked it within two feet from the hole, Hogan would say, "Get yourself another game, boy, you don't know how to play. You've got to come in left to right." With Hogan, you had to be able to shape your shots the right way.

Back when we played the Open in '66, he came down to my club, the California Golf Club, where I belonged, and we would practice there with no one around. He was someone that you watched. He was the greatest course manager I've ever seen. He told me all kinds of things about the Masters. He told me about the twelfth hole. He would talk with me like nobody else. And he always walked on my left. I can't remember him ever walking to my right. I don't know why. He just felt comfortable there. That's the way it was. Since Hogan would never walk to my right, if you'll notice me on the CBS Tower (at golf telecasts), I sit to every announcer's right. They are on my left. I feel comfortable talking to the left—it's just like talking to him.

———

Jack Tooke for many years was one of California's top amateur golfers, and he credits Hogan for being the mentor who took the time to turn him from being a very good golfer to a topnotch one, able to shoot consistently in the 60s. Tooke was not a long-time Hogan protégé—this all happened during one six-month period, while Hogan was spending one winter layoff in residence at Tamarisk Golf Club in Rancho Mirage, California, where, Tooke said, he was paid $100,000 as a touring pro in residence. Tooke, by the way, recently shot a 64 at the age of seventy-three:

I won a lot of amateur tournaments in California, but didn't do any of that until after I had played some golf with him. The one time I actually played a round of golf with him, I was eight under going to the sixteenth hole, then hit two balls out of bounds and shot 68. He had a 70. He was knocking them stiff but missing one putt after another, whereas I was making putts from all over the place. He told me I could be a great golfer, but I needed to change my stance and my grip to hit the ball straight. One thing he did was change my grip. I had a very strong grip and hooked everything, but I was able to get away with it because I was a great putter. Hogan straightened me out. He got me onto the practice tee and we did a lot of practicing. Still, it took me a long time to get my hands to where he wanted me to put them on the club. Once I got it, I could hit the ball really straight.

I was in my twenties at the time. He would see me hitting balls out there and come out to join me. He liked me. He wasn't really out there to give me lessons, but the kind of attention he gave me was something he didn't do for a lot of people. After he started changing my grip, I couldn't hit the ball hardly. I would shank everything, and this was after I had hooked everything. But at the time I was such a good putter I was able to make up for my wildness. All told, he ended up working with me for about six months. He would say, "You're doing it right, just pounding those balls every day."

He was a quiet person, even when he talked. He would stand off to the right of me on the practice tee, facing me from the side so he could see what I was doing with my swing. After a while, I got to where I could aim at the flag instead of always out to the right of it for my hook. He changed me to a weaker grip. It took me about three or four weeks to get the hang of it, but I finally conquered it. It was like I was starting golf all over again.

That winter at Tamarisk was not long after his accident. When he would go out to practice, he would bring all new balls with him to hit, and I would just sit there and watch. During his time there that year he played at a golf tournament at Thunderbird Country Club, and that was in the days when you could walk alongside players in the fairway. This particular time, I walked five or six holes with him side by side, and he didn't even know I was there. That's how focused he was. He would just walk along between shots with his head down, so he could concentrate better without being distracted.

That's not a sand trap Hogan is hitting out of at Olympic in the 1955 U.S. Open. It's a bunker, and he would be the first to correct you. (AP/Wide World Photos)

Finally, he noticed that the same pair of shoes had been near him the whole time, and that's when he looked up at me to see that I was there.

―――

*There were two things that tour golfers did at tournaments in which Hogan also played: They would practice on their own and play their rounds, then when word got out that Hogan was out practicing, run over to the practice tee to watch Hogan at work. Tommy Bolt supposedly once observed that while Jack Nicklaus would watch Hogan hit balls, you would never see Hogan watching Nicklaus. **Al Geiberger,** who broke onto the tour* *circa 1960, was among those wearing his "running shoes" when a Hogan Alert was issued:*

It was such a rare occasion because by the time I was coming out on tour, he was really starting to fade—to slow down and play only once in a while. We players used to talk about "the Secret" and wonder what it was. But I'm not so sure that anyone still really knows what his so-called secret was. He came out with his book *Five Lessons: The Modern Fundamentals of Golf*, which talks about good grip, good posture, etc. I guess you might say he was ahead of his time. Most of the teachers nowadays have caught up with him, which is why there are so many good players out on the regular tour that all look a lot alike—they all come out with these great fundamental swings. You look at the Senior PGA Tour and see where we have a lot of different swings. That's because guys came up with what you might call caddie swings. Hogan was one of those guys who plugged through and figured out a lot of things in this game.

———

John Mahaffey won an NCAA Championship and a PGA Championship, and struck up an enduring friendship with Ben Hogan even before he had gotten out of the University of Houston. As Mahaffey found out, there was more to being a Hogan apprentice than just getting practice-tee tips. Part of the process was being available for some friendly rounds of golf, and those rubbed off well on Mahaffey:

I played a lot of golf with him. The first time I met Ben Hogan was when I worked at Champions Golf Club (in

Houston) before I came out on the tour. We played two practice rounds prior to the last event he ever played, at Champions, in 1971. On the Sunday night prior to the Colonial—I was having dinner at the golf course—he came up to my table and said, "Would you like to play in Colonial next week?" And I said, "Mr. Hogan, I'm not a member of the tour or eligible to play at Colonial." And he said, "I didn't ask you that. I asked you if you wanted to play Colonial next week." And I said, "I'd love to." He said, "One stipulation: I want to play three practice rounds with you." I told him that would be great. He went away, made a phone call, came back to the table, and said, "You're in."

I think I shot 72 in a pretty good wind the first time we played at Champions, and he shot 71. He asked me if I wanted to play the next day, and I said I'd love to. We only got to play nine holes. We got abbreviated by a thunderstorm that lasted the rest of the afternoon. I shot a 32 on the front and he shot 31. We were playing for a little money, and I was struggling trying to get on tour, but he never took any money—he just said he enjoyed playing.

I then played three practice rounds with him at Colonial and ended up finishing something like ninth in the tournament, and I even had a chance to win it that year. He showed me a lot of (local knowledge) at Colonial, even though some of the things are a little out-dated now, and the golf ball didn't go quite as far. Like the first hole, a par-five of about 570 yards. He said never to shoot at the first green because it didn't make any sense: It was too big of a gamble and at that time the fair-ways weren't as good as they are now. Plus the greens were much harder and not quite as well manicured. He told me what clubs to hit on certain holes and where to hit it. It was fabulous. I played Colonial that way every year I played, and I think I finished second to Ben Crenshaw one year at Colonial and had several chances to win.

We became good friends. I played his equipment for about seventeen years out on the tour. We had a very nice relationship. He helped me some with my game, maybe not so much with what he said but with his attitude—just through osmosis, more or less, watching him hit balls and playing golf with him and catching his tempo and paying attention to what he did. I went out to Shady Oaks in Fort Worth a few times to hit balls and also watch him hit balls. I've played with a lot of what I consider great players, and I don't know to this day that I've ever seen anyone with as much control over the golf ball as he had. Some are awfully close, the Trevinos of the world and some others, but he was probably the best tee to green I've ever seen.

Hogan not only helped tour pros with their games and swing keys, he also helped others, such as his Fort Worth niece **Jacqueline Hogan Towery,** *who was his brother Royal's daughter:*

As a child I was supposed to carry on the Hogan name and tradition and play golf. So Uncle Ben gave me lessons at Colonial Country Club. I tried hard to succeed at the family sport, but I'm afraid that I wasn't very good.

At least I wasn't as good as Ben thought I should be, so one day he suggested that I might want to find something else to do. Later, before he got so ill and when we were eating at Shady Oaks, he told me he had a secret swing that he could teach me, and I could beat anyone. Unfortunately, he never taught me the swing. Maybe he is sharing that with God.

———

When he gave swing tips, Hogan was very hands-on. When he really wanted to get a point across, he would reach for a belt— not to whip with, but to use as a makeshift swing-aid device. On one particular occasion, it was Hogan's Shady Oaks roundtable buddy **Bob Wynne** *who had to reach for his belt:*

Whenever I'd come in after playing, I knew he would chew me out about something. I hated coming into nine and eighteen because he was always watching. One time I glanced over there, and sure enough he was giving me the motion to come over. He turned his chair around and he said, "Take your belt off."

"Well, Mr. Hogan, if I do that my pants will fall down."

He was serious. "Bob, take your belt off." So I took my belt off. Then he said, "Hold your elbows together, like this." So I did, and he took that belt and tied it around just above the elbows. Now this was before all these contraptions came out. Then he said, "Now go out and hit balls until your hands bleed."

One of my buddies was standing there with me. I didn't take the belt off my arms. I went back out there and my friend teed my ball up for me. I had a six-iron in my hand. I tried to hit the ball, but I could hardly get around. About the third time, I finally hit it, and I was just trying to concentrate on getting back, hitting the ball, and everything. That ball went out there about 155 yards straighter than a string. It was just amazing to me. I went to the range and then he explained the whole thing to me like he was a physics teacher or something. My backswing was too far, my elbows were flying, etc. He taught me from that lesson that you have to keep your elbows close together. It's hard to do, yeah, but once you realize you can do it, it helps. It cut down on my big looping backswing, so it made my clubhead speed on the downswing faster and I kept my eye on the ball better.

Even though Hogan was the master of the impromptu lesson, he was sometimes willing to take on a golfer as a long-term project, as was the case with Fort Worth oilman and Hogan country-club pal **Tex Moncrief,** *who says:*

He was a great player, no question about that. Back in about 1954 when he was right at the top of the game, he said, "I'm going to make a golfer out of you and I want you to come over to Colonial when I practice," which was two o'clock or something—after he had practiced for two or three hours, and he probably had already practiced in the morning, too. He got me out there and showed me some things and would get me to practice with him, starting with the nine-iron or something like that. He told me to just hit the ball and try to take a neat divot and then just keep going backward or a little bit forward where you just dig out a hole. Every time he would take a divot he'd move the ball back just a little bit to where he could take another bite of grass out.

It was one of the greatest things that ever happened to me concerning my golf game. I practiced with Ben for about four days. We started out one Monday. Darned if on Thursday night I get a phone call at home. I got up from the dining room table—we had a floor without a carpet on it, so we had a rug in there—and I slipped and hit my left side and broke a couple of ribs. I cracked them and, hell, they didn't heal for three months. So I never did get to finish my series of lessons with Ben, but I still remember it and what a kick I got out of it. My game was pretty well built by then, and all the bad strokes that I had were built into my game. But Ben changed me around in the way I played and showed me certain things to do, and it was helping the heck out of me. I will always regret I didn't get to finish it. It was something that you couldn't have paid for; he just wanted to do it. And some people would have given a left arm just to get thirty minutes with him. The last ten years of his life, he took Kris Tschetter (of the LPGA) under his wing, and before her there was a guy from the PGA Tour named Tom Byrum.

Tom Byrum has been a PGA Tour regular since 1986. He won the Kemper Open in 1989 and has notched a slew of top-ten finishes since then. Byrum bears somewhat of a physical resemblance to a young Hogan, and his squared-off flat swing demonstrates elements of the classic Hogan swing. Byrum played out of Hogan's club, Shady Oaks in Fort Worth, for a

*number of years, during which time he got to spend countless
hours learning from the Great One:*

He was a competitor. I could tell that just by the passion
he had when he helped me. He would always tell me to
find an edge or advantage on the course that wasn't obvious to other players. And he would always tell me to
"outwork 'em." I remember coming back from a bad
stretch of weeks on tour and was walking through the
men's grill; Hogan always sat with his back to the room
looking out the window where he could see the tenth tee
and the ninth and eighteenth greens. When he saw me
come in to get a drink he got up and waved me over. I
walked over, and he asked me why my scores had been so
bad. I told him I wasn't hitting it well, and he started in
on a pep talk that wasn't technical at all but inspiring. I
was pumped after a five-minute speech that ended with
"Now get your country ass out there and outwork 'em!"
Needless to say, when he stared you down with his ice
blue eyes, you knew he meant what he was saying!

---

*Asking Hogan for help out of the blue usually got the same
response, which 1999 Senior PGA Tour rookie phenom* **Bruce
Fleisher** *can vouch for:*

I was doing a couple of corporate outings in Fort Worth
after the Colonial Tournament one year, and I remember
asking him questions about the golf swing. He said, "Bruce,
do yourself a favor: Go out there for two weeks, eight hours
a day, and I'll bet you when you come back, you won't
have to ask me that question again." Which means, go

find it out for yourself. He was a man of a few words. He basically was saying, "I did it on my own. You go do it on your own," which basically really isn't a bad way to go. I also remember him telling me that he never played a round of golf where he didn't go over every shot in his mind the night before. That's the way he managed his golf.

———

Hogan was a man of few words, even when dispensing advice to those few professional golfers he allowed inside his inner circle. But then there was the occasional exception to the rule, such as when **Kermit Zarley,** *now playing the Senior PGA Tour, got into a lengthy discussion with Hogan at Shady Oaks, an exchange that was as technical as it was revelatory to Zarley, because it helped him understand why he had been suffering from neck problems for years:*

A few years after I had played at Champions in 1971with Hogan during his fateful (next-to-last competitive) round, I was headed to play in the Colonial over in Fort Worth, when one of my friends, Wally Armstrong, said, "Hey, let's go over to Shady Oaks and watch Hogan practice, because everyone knows that he practices over there in the morning. Let's bring our shag balls, too." That's because in those days—this was 1979—you were still hitting your own shag balls on the practice range. Wally said, "I know the pro and I've already called over there, and he says we can practice on the par-three course where Hogan practices." So that's what we did. Sure enough, Hogan was there and there were already some pros watching him. Two of them I can remember were Ken Still and Bruce Devlin.

Most people who knew Hogan and knew his reputation didn't try to talk to him half the time—they just watched him. As I was watching him, and I don't know if he remembered that he and I had played together a few years earlier at Champions, I could see from watching him that Hogan was still pretty sharp. I just started asking him some questions about the swing, which a lot of pros were reluctant to do because of his reputation, but I did anyway. He was real nice to me and answered my questions and so forth. Then Wally and I went down about thirty or fifty yards away and started hitting our own balls. I soon learned that Hogan was standing up where he was watching me hit, and he said something to Bruce Devlin about my swing. So Devlin walked over to me and said, "Hogan said something about your swing. You ought to go over there and ask him about it—he never does this."

I walked over to Ben and said, "Bruce said you said something about my swing—would you care to tell me about it?" He was standing at a ninety-degree angle from my line of flight, looking face on at me. He said, "When you finish your swing, your elbow is going way past your neck. You shouldn't do that." I said to him, "That is amazing to me that you would say that. You are the first person who has ever said that to me in my life. But even more amazing to me is that I've just begun to think that is what has been causing all my neck trouble." And he said, "What neck trouble?" I said, "Well, four years ago I had a neck fusion—two vertebrae were fused after six years of neck trouble."

I don't think he quite understood everything I said right away, but here's what he said, and it was a perfect moment with his sarcasm: "Well, it looks to me like if a man's golf swing is causing him to break his neck he would change it." I told him I was just beginning to figure it out. I had asked doctors all the time, "Hey, is my golf swing causing my neck trouble?" And every one of them said no, but there was no sports medicine in those days to speak of. I was figuring this out myself, and I thought I was putting a strain on my neck because my left arm was going way around. They call that a block.

Hogan and I got into a real deep discussion about the golf swing. And I said to him, "Well, actually this is the reason I asked you earlier if you tried to keep your right elbow in tight in your backswing," and he had said, "No, I try to keep it low." There had always been these rumors circulating around in pro golf about what Hogan did in order to keep his right elbow in tight: One rumor was that he put a ball underneath his armpit and swung, without the ball dropping in his backswing or his downswing. Hogan had an extremely flat backswing, and when he swung it looked like he forced his right elbow in close to his body. He wrote some stuff in his main book, *Five Lessons*, which related to this, but he never said it that way. I explained to him that the reason my left elbow swings around like that, which is a blocky action in your follow-through—your upswing—is because it related to what I had asked him about. Here's what I do in my backswing: I get through the top of my backswing and my clubhead starts to drop inside of my backswing plane. And on the downswing, it drops more, so that I create two different planes, and the downswing plane of the clubhead is considerably inside the backswing plane of the clubhead. And he said, "What's wrong with that?"

Now, I was not at all surprised that he said that. I knew what he believed in. He believes in two different planes—a backswing plane and a downswing plane, and he wants the clubhead's downswing plane inside his backswing plane. So I said, "That would be great—if I did that and my hands went the same way." Visualize two planes on the backswing—a plane made by your clubhead and a plane made by your hands—and you also visualize two planes on your downswing, one made by your clubhead and one made by your hands. I said, "If my hand plane went the same way with my clubhead plane on the backswing, and if my hands are inside on my downswing and my clubhead is inside on my downswing, that would be great." (I know this very well, because I've taken more movies of the golf swing than any pro on tour has taken.) I then said, "My clubhead drops inside, but my hands go to the outside at the start of my downswing. I raise the hands out of the plane, and they go right over the top, but the clubhead still drops to the inside and it sets up a different shaft angle. Every single time a person does that, they shut the face of the club. That's what I do. So that when I come down into the ball, I'm going to hit the ball left, if I don't block with the left arm. That's why I block with the left arm." When I said that, he said to me, "I don't know everything there is to know about the golf swing, I don't think anybody does." Those were his exact words.

I discovered sometime after this conversation with Hogan that he had hit on exactly what had caused all my neck pain. There were some people on the tour before this that were teaching a folding of the left arm on the upswing—George Knudson, for example—and they probably got it from watching Hogan. At any rate, it was that, and I began to discover that the reasons my backswing problems were like that were, primarily, because I had tried to force my right elbow in this way all of my life, and I thought that was the right way to swing the club. The thing that always mystified me was Jack Nicklaus's swing because Nicklaus had a flying right elbow and it stuck way out behind him. Nowadays, you have Tom Kite, Tom Watson, and Fred Couples—all great players—and all of them do this. All of my life, swing instructors had said, "A flying right elbow is terrible in golf," and they used to criticize Nicklaus's swing for this. They're absolutely wrong. There's nothing wrong with a flying right elbow. In fact, here's what a flying right elbow does: You'll never see a man who swings the club back and sticks the elbow behind him, like Jack Nicklaus does, who has the same kind of trouble I do, which is to drop the clubhead to the inside on the downswing with the hands going over the top and shutting the club(head). That's some of the stuff I learned about the golf swing and talking to Hogan got me thinking and learning a whole lot more about it.

LPGA tour veteran **Kris Tschetter** *joined Shady Oaks with her family in the early eighties, and within several years she had become one of Hogan's pet teaching projects:*

At first, when Mr. Hogan came up and said, "Let me see you hit a few," I was obviously pretty nervous. But I got real comfortable with it. I was always very comfortable around him. I think we had a relationship where I understood his sense of humor. People were so afraid and nervous around him, that when he said something funny, people didn't know how to react. He was really very, very funny, and he would just crack me up.

During my first year on tour, I was coming home from my last tournament of the year and had about four days before I had to go back to Q School, when my clubs got stolen. So there I was scrambling around, trying to get my clubs back together. At the time I was hitting a Taylor Made driver with a graphite shaft, which Mr. Hogan just thought was the worst. So I got a new set of irons and was waiting for two new sand wedges to come. Meanwhile, Mr. Hogan had given me a bunch of drivers to try.

My new driver from Taylor Made arrived, and I put it in my bag with those drivers Mr. Hogan had given me.

Large crowds followed Hogan everywhere he went, but few knew much about him beyond his swing. (Jules Alexander photo)

So now I've got a ton of drivers in my bag trying to figure out which one I was going to use, plus I'm waiting for these sand wedges. Mr. Hogan comes out and he's watching me hit, and I'm thinking, "I'm not pulling the Taylor Made driver out until after he leaves." Normally, he would come out for about an hour, or an hour and a half, but this time he stayed for what seemed like forever. He wasn't going to leave. Finally, I knew I had to hit this driver, so I pulled it out and he says to me, "What's that?" I started laughing and I told him, "This is my Taylor Made driver." He goes (imitating Hogan in gruff voice), "Taylor Made, huh? Why don't you get Mr. Taylor to get you some sand wedges." At this point, most people would really be upset, but I just started laughing and said, "I can't believe you. I play with thirteen of your clubs in my bag and you're going to get mad because I have one Taylor Made?" He just laughs and says, "All right, let me see that buggy whip." And we just went on. I knew that he was joking. He would definitely bait me and tease me. He would absolutely crack me up.

When I was with him, I didn't look at him as Ben Hogan, legend, but just as a fun person who had all this knowledge about golf. His big key to being a champion was outworking everyone. That was the thing he harped on—outthink them and outwork them.

We were very different personalities on the golf course. I focus when I'm hitting my shot, but I'm everywhere else when I'm walking down the fairway. I can talk to people in the gallery, where he would just stay focused the whole time. And I'm much more aggressive than he was. He was very, very careful and didn't take unnecessary chances. Of course, when you hit it as well as he did, course management comes pretty easily. But I learned from him to be cautious in some circumstances. If I hadn't spent time with him, I'd probably be more reckless than I am. There was never any one thing he told me that [meant], "This is what you've got to do." It came through conversations. I can't pinpoint where I learned what I learned. It almost seems kind of ingrained now, and that's from spending time with him.

Hogan, as mentor, could be tough as nails. As Ryder Cup captain, most recently in 1967, he tightened the strings even more, as 1967 U.S. team member **Johnny Pott** *remembers:*

We were having a Ryder Cup team meeting (in 1967) during the Colonial tournament in preparation for that year's Ryder Cup match to be played at Champions in Houston. The ten-man team had already been determined, and this was only the second time that a nonplaying captain would be elected for the team. The last playing captain we had was on the '63 team and that was Arnold Palmer. The thought was to honor past PGA champions by making them captain of the Ryder Cup.

The first nonplaying captain was Byron Nelson, when the match was being played at Royal Birkdale. Ben Hogan was playing in the Colonial that year, and we felt that if there was ever an opportunity to have Hogan be the nonplaying captain, it would be at Champions because he was such good friends with Jimmy Demaret and Jackie Burke. I don't know exactly how I was chosen to be the one to ask him if he would be the captain, but

I guess I was unanimously elected to do that—which probably meant that I was the last man on the team or something like that.

Hogan was not playing much when I came out as a rookie, except for just an occasional tournament. I did play one practice round with him, Jay Hebert, and Gardner Dickinson during the Doral Tournament in Miami. Like so many of the other golfers, I was in awe around Ben Hogan. I never really knew what to call him. I certainly wasn't familiar enough to call him Ben, and I didn't want to call him Mr. Hogan, because I thought that might make him think I was being a smarty. So I'd call him something like "Hey, Mr. Ben Hogan," or whatever.

Anyhow, I went out from the meeting to find him, and I found him in the locker room. I approached him and I probably said, "Mr. Ben Hogan, I'm Johnny Pott." I didn't know if he had any idea who I was, even though just a couple of years earlier at Colonial I had tied Arnold Palmer, and Arnold beat me in an eighteen-hole playoff on Monday. I said, "I'm a member of the current Ryder Cup team and the team would like for you to be our captain at the matches at Houston in September." And he says, "Uh. Champions, huh? September, huh? . . . I'll let you know tomorrow." And I said, "Well, I really would appreciate a positive answer because it would just be an honor for you to be our captain." I went back up to the meeting with the PGA and the rest of the players and relayed the story to them. They said, "We'll just have to wait and find out tomorrow."

It worked out at the Colonial tournament that I had opposite tee times with Mr. Hogan. At Colonial, you walk out of the locker room through the pro shop to get to the first tee or the practice tee or whatever. Next day I was going out of the locker room and he's coming in, and as we passed, he says, "I'll do it." A man of very few words. He never broke his stride as he looked me in the eye. That was all I heard from him, so I reported that to the PGA and the rest of the players that Ben said he would do it.

Hogan was a totally different captain than Byron Nelson had been. Byron wrote us a letter every week and kept us informed and all that. Byron was very outgoing and kept us abreast of everything that was happening. And maybe that had been because we were going to England for the (1965) matches. But we really never did hear much from Hogan, except we knew from our correspondence from the PGA that he definitely was going to be there.

We were told to arrive in Houston on the Monday of Ryder Cup week. There were ten players on the team, and we were told to be there on Monday for a practice round. Normally, what we would do was play two five-somes. Well, we were getting ready to play about ten o'clock and Arnold Palmer hadn't arrived. Hogan goes around to everyone and asks, "Where is Arnold Palmer?" Somebody said, "Well, he's not here yet. We haven't seen him." Hogan says, "I'm gonna wait a little while. I really want us all to play in two fivesomes, and I'd like to see how you guys are playing." About a half an hour later, Arnold buzzed us at Champions in his jet. He flew by about five hundred feet above the ground, made some funny turns and all that kind of stuff. Hogan looks up and says, "Oh, there's Arnold Palmer, huh?" There's an air-port in the vicinity of Champions where Arnold landed, and I think Arnie got a citation from the FAA for buzzing the golf course. But that's another story.

Arnold shows up and he walks out on the practice tee hitching his pants, and you know how Arnold is, and he says, "Hey, Ben, what ball are we playing?" Hogan says, "Well, Mr. Palmer, when you make the team, I'll let you know." He was pretty hot at Arnold for not being there with the rest of us.

We finally get on the tee. You know, it's kind of hard to hit your golf ball when you're looking Hogan in the eye. Some of us were intimidated playing in front of him. He was staring every one of us down. I don't know what he was looking at and thinking, but the way he looked at me kind of gave me the feeling that he was thinking, "How in the world did this guy ever make five cents on the tour with a swing like that?" When you've got the master looking at you, you're trying to make a pretty good swing. So I made a couple of funny old fast swings and finally I just went over to him and I said—by then I was calling him "Ben" because we had been told to call him Ben—"Ben, would you come along with me for a couple of holes and just watch me hit every shot?" So we played maybe the first two holes at Champions and then the next thing you know we played the third hole and he was there but I didn't even notice him. So I got used to him.

After we practiced, he said, "I want you boys who drive the ball straight playing together. You boys who drive long and crooked, I'm going to put you together. Gene Littler never could play one of your second shots, Johnny, from over there in the woods." So he paired Bobby Nichols and myself together. I'd had occasion to hit a crooked ball every now and then, and that's what happens when you hit 'em hard. But we killed them. And I think Bobby and I both were 4-and-0 for the matches.

In the team meeting, the first thing he said to the guys was, "You know, I never was comfortable playing in anybody else's clothes." And, of course, on the Ryder Cup we had these uniforms and everybody was supposed to dress like a team. "You fellows can wear whatever you want. And (Doug) Sanders, if you want to come out here dressed like a peacock, you just go right ahead and make yourself comfortable. But let me tell you one thing. I don't want my name on that trophy as the losing captain."

One other thing that happened was that he was the first Ryder Cup captain to introduce his team in an opening ceremony or function as "the greatest ten players in the world." I thought that might intimidate the team from Great Britain.

Champions had a first hole on the Cypress Creek course that was a par-four dogleg left—kind of down and to the left. You know how festive the Ryder Cup is. Well, it was a foggy morning and on the green the marine band started playing all those songs, like "The Star Spangled Banner" and "God Save the Queen," and marching up that fairway in the fog. Somebody said, "God, Ben, who's going to hit the first ball?" He says, "No doubt about it: Gene (Littler) is first. He don't give a crap about nothing."

A number of golfers have played Hogan clubs over the years, although membership in that fraternity never carried with it a guarantee that Hogan would be your friend or even your part-time swing guru. Sometimes all a Hogan-club player could hope for was to play a round or two with Hogan and see if anything rubbed off, as **Charles Coody** *set about to do after he turned professional in 1963:*

The first time I met him was when I signed with the Hogan Company to play their clubs after I had turned professional. As far as I know he didn't approach people: In my case, that was left to the president of the company. If you represented his company, he expected you to play with his equipment and that's the way it should be. Some guys today don't play everything they're supposed to play.

I was with the company for the first two years or so I was on the tour, and I played with him a couple of times in practice during that time. I also played with him maybe three or four times in tournaments, which was pretty unusual because there was so much difference in our ages. Playing with him was very intimidating, as anyone would expect—he was just such an imposing figure. At times he played as though he was the best player who had ever played. Knowing that, you were scared to hit a bad shot around him. But he was a pleasure to play with, always a gentleman.

I'd watch him practice sometimes at Shady Oaks or Rivercrest, and it was like watching a machine. The caddie could almost take a chair, sit down out there, and reach over and pick up the balls, no matter what club Hogan was hitting. And you'd think to yourself, "If that's what I've got to do to be good, then how in the world do I ever get there?" I never tried to emulate Hogan because he faded the ball, and I turned it right to left. I grew up in

167

a small town in west Texas and I had a homemade swing like a lot of kids did at that time. Whether it was good or it was bad, I never really tried to tinker with it like a lot of people do with their swings today. We didn't have the video and stuff to work with like they do now. I never saw my swing on film until I was in my early twenties.

———

Those closest to Hogan said he mellowed a bit in later life and went out of his way to give lessons to amateur golfers, even when they wouldn't expect it. But if you worked or played at Shady Oaks and caught Hogan's eye, there always was a chance that he would ask you to show him your swing, or at least your grip, as head waiter **Charlie Hudson** *found out for himself:*

He changed over the years; he became friendlier in talking to people and giving them golf lessons. He had me swinging up there and all that. He taught me how to hold my hands and all that kind of stuff. In his later years, he would see somebody out there playing golf and not swinging the club back right. He'd go out there and show them how to hold the club and all that. Even little kids would be passing by and he'd go out if they had some clubs. He would say, "Let me see you swing." He liked kids. They would swing and he would work with them for a while.

We once had a girl working at the bar and he would talk about getting her a set of golf clubs. Eventually, he gave her a set of clubs and balls, and taught her how to play golf. He was pretty generous. People didn't hear about stuff like that a lot.

———

Of course, if you were a pro golfer and wanted to get an audience with Hogan, it was always helpful to be playing his clubs. Then there was Tom Weiskopf, the 1973 British Open champion, who was able to win Hogan over to his side even though he was playing MacGregors. Hogan had a little bit of extra patience with Weiskopf during a time that Weiskopf was in need. Hogan confidant **Gene Smyers** *retells the story:*

There were a lot of pros seeking Ben's counsel for help with their clubs. There was the story of Tom Weiskopf, who lost his clubs—the airline lost his clubs. He was playing MacGregor clubs. In desperation, he called Ben and he came in here and went to the Hogan Company. They didn't make a set of clubs. Instead, Weiskopf got with the people in the plant and with Ben and they gave him his specs on a set of irons. And Hogan said, "You take that to MacGregor and have them make the irons according to your specs." Well, they did. And Tom played with them and he was very happy, and this was at the peak of his career. Then the airlines lost his clubs again. So he called Ben a second time and the Hogan Company had apparently kept those specs. Ben again sent the specs to him and told him to tell Mr. MacGregor to keep these specs, because "This is the last time I am doing this."

———

For those pro golfers he really cared for, Hogan would sometimes go the extra mile on their behalf, as he did for **Ken Venturi** *when it seemed that Venturi wouldn't get an invite back for his second Masters in the mid-fifties:*

I met him in 1954, when I was paired with him in the second round of the Masters. I was in the service at the time. I qualified in '54 to play in '55, but I was overseas in the service. So I couldn't play. I couldn't use my exemption. I had gotten in in '54 because of my being on the Walker Cup team. In those days the Masters gave the Masters champions and the Open champions a vote to vote in somebody who was not otherwise invited to the Masters. So Hogan and those others went to them and said, "Hey, he qualified to play in '55, but he was in the service like a bunch of us had been, so he didn't have a chance to fulfill his exemption. I suggest that we vote him in." And all of the past Masters champions voted me in in 1956.

Some of Hogan's best lessons to golfers were given in as few words as possible, as **Tom Byrum** *explains following a short story he tells of the time he and fellow golf pro Kris Tschetter had the pleasure of joining Hogan for a few holes of golf:*

The most surprising thing I saw Hogan do was right after I first met him. Kris Tschetter and I were out playing nine and came up on Hogan playing a couple holes on his walk. He would carry one club and about five or six balls, stopping to hit them whenever he felt like it. Kris knew him better at the time and asked him to join us. To our surprise he did. He used my clubs and termed my driver a "quirk." He asked me if I knew what that was and I said no. He told me that's what they used to call a buggy whip. We played about four holes with him that day and

I would be willing to bet that is the last time he played with anyone again.

There was a time he would stop during his walks before going home to watch me hit balls. He had been doing this for three or four days in a row. He would stop, watch me hit a few shots, tell me to try this or that, and then watch me for a while longer before continuing on his way. One day my car needed some work, so I was late getting to practice. When Hogan came around, he stopped and watched a few, then asked, "Just get here?" I didn't know how he knew, but I said yes and continued to hit. A few minutes later he asked me what had held me up until this late in the day. I told him about my car and continued to hit, ready to try whatever he was going to suggest. Again after a couple of quiet moments he asked, "You got a bike?" I said I did, and he said, "Could've rode that out here." I agreed, ready to get on with the lesson, but again a few quiet moments. Then, "You could have walked, couldn't you?" I said, "Yes, I guess I could have." Now I'm sure he was done ripping me and that now he would help me with my swing. Well, after a few more quiet moments, I finally looked up to see why he wasn't giving me any tips. He was about a hundred yards away, walking toward the clubhouse. I got the point. You don't get his help because you're there. You get it when you've earned it!

———

Marty Leonard didn't get or solicit much golfing help from Hogan, a Leonard family friend, but she knew that Hogan held her in warm esteem. As for the golf lessons, Hogan put in some extra time trying to help Marvin Leonard, Marty's father, with his swing, as Marty points out:

We obviously had a close relationship. He gave me a little golf club, a pin. And on it, it says, "BH to ML." And he gave that to me when I was a young girl. It was given to me either at Christmas or on my birthday. I don't know exactly. Needless to say, I treasure it and I've still got it.

I think he probably took an interest in me because I was my father's daughter. Also, I was a pretty good golfer and he liked that. He didn't give Daddy much golf instruction. Daddy was a good golfer in his own way, but he had a very loosie-goosie kind of swing, and I remember that the few times Ben would try to help Daddy he would say, "Gosh, just hit the ball. Don't just swing at it, hit the ball." I don't think they got very far there, but they had many discussions about it through the years.

I'm sure Daddy sought Ben's advice, particularly when he was building Shady Oaks. Of course, Colonial was a different story. I don't think he probably helped as much with that. But I know he did with Shady Oaks. There were some trees he wanted to cut down and some things he wanted to do—some you did and some you didn't do. They all had their own distinct ideas and I think the golf course got built the way Daddy and architect (Robert) Trent Jones wanted it. But I think he sought his input on things, for sure. I know they talked and I could hear them.

⚊⚊

*Most of Hogan's longtime Shady Oaks cronies never really played that much golf with him, but that didn't exempt them from the occasional quick tip of stern correction, as **Dr. Jim Murphy,** Hogan's personal physician, and **Dee Kelly,** Hogan's attorney, found out over time:*

Dr. Murphy: I played one time with him. He was very quiet and he usually pretty much rode alone. When you'd fix up a game, you would try to get some handicaps here or some shots there. I don't think he ever gave a lot of strokes to anybody. He was very intent, even when he was just playing a leisure game. He didn't screw around, although he was a pleasure to play with. And I'd oftentimes go up there and practice before I played on Wednesday, and he'd be sitting down there in the tavern watching. When I'd come in, he would take me aside and

Hogan taught those he trusted how to look for an edge on the golf course, even if it meant taking a little extra time studying a putt, as he does here at the 1959 U.S. Open at Winged Foot. (Jules Alexander photo)

tell me how he thought I could improve my game and swing. He did that frequently. He'd say, "You don't take the club back far enough." And he was great on prona- tion. He would take you, and he'd get behind you and say (in a low, growling voice), "This is the way I want you to do it." He would almost break your arms.

Dee Kelly: I don't play a lot of golf, mostly weekend golf, in fact, and I remember having a hard time getting out of sand traps. I told him that, and he said to me, "Those are not sand traps; they're bunkers." He took me outside and then gave me a lesson to help me get out of a bunker. He told me to open up the clubface and hit in the sand behind the ball. I've since been able to get out of bunkers pretty well.

5

HOGAN, THE MONEYMAN

Ben believed that the tough times were what made him what he was, and he often said that without those experiences he could not have made it as a golfer.

—JACQUELINE HOGAN TOWERY

Ben Hogan was far from being a golf savant. The same qualities that made him one of the best golfers of all time—hard work and focus—made him a natural businessman. He was multifaceted, and he had a nose for business. When he was still at the peak of his competitive career, he started the Ben Hogan Golf Company with partner Pollard Simons. This was between 1953 and 1954. The company overcame an early glitch or two to emerge as one of the golf industry's leaders in the manufacture of golf clubs. Hogan clubs were popular with topnotch golfers and the wealthy: JFK's set of clubs that were auctioned off for about $1 million in the 1990s were Hogans.

Hogan was no mere figurehead at his company, even after it had been sold several times between 1960 and 1993. He demanded the most out of a workforce that at one time grew to almost five hundred. It wasn't all smooth sailing. When $100,000 worth of the company's initial inventory rolled off the assembly line, Hogan took one look at the finished product and decided it just was not good enough. Simons, confident that they actually did have quality product, wanted to go ahead and sell the clubs. Hogan reportedly preempted that move by cutting the heads off all the clubs. So instead of selling them at a reduced rate, Hogan trashed the clubs and told his staff to start over. That move nearly sank the company, but Hogan eventually got new backing guaranteed by long-time supporter Marvin Leonard (and, later, Bing Crosby, among others), and the Hogan Company was back on its feet.

Hogan had all but retired from golf by the mid-1950s. In 1960 he sold the Hogan Company to American Machine and Foundry (AMF). That made him a wealthy man, if not a retiring one, and Hogan parlayed much of what he made off the sale into investments in the oil business. All the while, Hogan maintained an office at the company that continued to bear his name and dropped by for at least part of the workday until another sale of the company, back to AMF, Inc., in 1993, resulted in moving the headquarters from Fort Worth to Virginia. By this time, Hogan was well entrenched in the oil business, purchasing properties with the help and counsel of oil-savvy friends. He had his share of busts but also his share of hits, and it's fair to say that he and Valerie were sitting on a nest egg well into seven figures at the time of their respective deaths.

Hogan didn't just lend his name and reputation to business—he jumped right into the middle of whatever he invested in, and took great pains to learn as much as he could about any of his endeavors. He often asked penetrating questions and he never forgot the business side of running a pro shop, something he had done years earlier during his days as a touring pro. When all was said and done, Hogan was as much a moneyman when it came to business as he had been coming down the back nine at a Masters or U.S. Open.

---

*Hogan acquired an appreciation for hard work and business at an early age, starting when he joined older brother Royal Hogan in delivering newspapers in their hometown of Fort Worth. Royal's daughter and Ben's niece, **Jacqueline Hogan Towery**, offers this brief history lesson:*

My father (Royal Hogan) quit school in the sixth grade and went to work to help support the family. Daddy sold the *Fort Worth Star-Telegram* newspaper at the Texas and Pacific Railroad Station in the south end of downtown. The paper probably sold for less than a nickel, so you can imagine how much money he made. Daddy got the papers, and he would give Ben some to sell, but my father always took the best spot for selling. He would sell out first, then go help Ben sell his papers. I was told that the old canvas bag he used to carry the papers was as big as Ben himself.

Royal and Ben were very much like all young boys, sometimes doing things they knew would get them in trouble. When they had sold all of their newspapers, they would carry passengers' luggage to make extra money. Only Red Caps were allowed to do this, and one day, each boy carrying a bag in each hand, they were caught by a Red Cap. Running as fast as they could with such a load, they realized that they could not outrun the Red Cap. They dropped the bags on the spot and just kept running until they were out of the station. That was the end of the extra money for carrying bags. After the papers were sold, sometimes near midnight, they would go up Main Street to the corner of Third and Main and get a hamburger for five cents.

This is the type of story they loved to share over and over. Although times were very tough, they enjoyed remembering them. Ben believed that the tough times were what made him what he was, and he often said that without those experiences he could not have made it as a professional golfer. And although Daddy never said it, I'm sure that the hard times contributed to his successful career in business.

A good businessman is a man of honor, and that's a quality that **Ken Venturi** *bestows on Hogan:*

Ben was a man of his word. My father was a man of his word, too. My father said you can break any contract in the world, but you can't break your handshake or your word. When it was spoken, you could never break that. And that was of Ben Hogan. I mean, his handshake or his word was his bond.

We got to know each other because a lot of the people that I knew were investors in the Hogan Company. I worked for Eddie Lowery and he was an investor and so were men like George Coleman, Paul Shields, and Marvin Leonard. That's kind of how Hogan got with me in '54. We had talked and everything, and that's the first time he told me to call him Ben—that was on the second hole of the Masters in '54.

In '58—I had turned pro in '56—I still hadn't signed with a company. I hadn't signed on for any clubs or balls. I was playing MacGregor clubs, and MacGregor wanted to sign me, but that meant I would have to play their ball and I didn't like the ball. There wasn't that much money in it anyway, so I wanted to play the best equipment. Ben made me an offer to sign with his company. He didn't have anybody on his staff. I was the only one he wanted to pay to be on his staff. And he offered me a price. It wasn't very much at all, but they didn't have any money. And I said, "Let me think about it," and he said, "Before you do anything, will you give me a call before you make a decision?" And I said, "Ben, you've got my word. You can bet I'll call you."

Months went by and I got approached by U.S. Royal. I didn't have to play their clubs: I could play my own clubs. And they offered me five times what Hogan had offered me. Not that it was that much, but it was quite a bit in those days, . . . even though what you got then you can get for one-day outings nowadays. Well, the head of U.S. Royal, John Sproul, came to San Francisco to Eddie Lowery's office and he brought the contract in the afternoon to Eddie's office.

So John Sproul says to sign it, but I said, "I've got to call Ben Hogan first and tell him what I'm going to do and give him a shot." So we called Ben's office. I talked to his secretary and she said he was not in. She thought he was at Shady Oaks or someplace like that. I said, "Well, could you track him down?" They couldn't find him. I said, "Please tell him I'm calling and I'm trying to get ahold of him." She said, "Okay, as soon as I find him, I'll have him call you." I said, "Thank you very much." At that time, U.S. Royal also made the Ben Hogan ball.

I said, "I can't sign because I haven't gotten ahold of Hogan."

Sproul said, "What's the difference? Sign here, and then tell him tomorrow, because he can't match this price. So just sign, 'cause I've gotta leave."

"John, I can't find him. I gave Ben my word."

"Well, you could lose this contract."

"John, if I lose it, I lose it, but I'm not breaking my word to Ben Hogan."

He stayed overnight, and the next morning we called Ben's office and he was there. I told him what the price was, and he said, "Ken, I can't match it, but thank you for calling." I then told him, "I didn't want to sign the contract until I spoke to you." And he said, "Is John Sproul there?" And I said, "Yeah." He said, "Let me speak to him."

So John takes the phone and says to Hogan, "Let me tell you what this dummy guy did. He said he wouldn't sign the contract because he gave you his word and that he wouldn't sign anything until he spoke to you first, and he could have blown the contract. I was going to leave town and I was going to say the heck with it, you don't have a contract, and he said, 'Fine, go.' " So he is talking and I don't hear Hogan, of course, and Sproul said, "No, I'm not kidding you. This guy was adamant. He was ready to blow the contract because he gave you his word."

I get back on the phone and he says, "Ken, that means a lot to me. That is really something. Your loyalty and dedication and your word has meant a lot. I want you to know something: If there is anything you ever need or ever want in this world of golf or anything else I can do, you call on me first." And that's where we cemented our bond.

———

When Hogan ever had any business questions to be answered or problems to be solved, he always had a platoon of contacts he could call on, such as Fort Worth oilman **Tex Moncrief:**

When he was going to start his golf-equipment company, my dad was in California. We were leaving Rivercrest one evening and I said, "Ben, my dad wanted you to know that we would all go in and back you if you wanted to build some golf clubs"—my dad and a fellow named Ed Landreth and two or three others that he knew. "My dad wanted me to tell you that." And he said, "Well, I thank you and appreciate it, but I'm going to go in with Pollard Simons." Pollard Simons was a fellow from Dallas that did go in with Ben on the golf clubs to start with. But they fell out, and that's when Marvin Leonard took him out and backed him. And they did all right, and then he sold out to AMF.

One time after he sold out, he showed up at the club, where my dad had a locker straight across from Ben's locker. Ben was reading one of AMF's annual reports. Seeing this, my dad said to Hogan, "I just want to tell you one thing. You don't have to read those reports, but that stock you've got in AMF? You ought to sell about half of it and put the money in good government bonds or something else good. Take the profit." AMF went way up, but Ben didn't sell any of it and then it went way down. Of course, he eventually sold some of it.

—————

Doxie Williams spent thirteen years as Hogan's personal administrative assistant at the Hogan Company, where, as could be expected, she was kept busy guarding her boss's time:

He was never there for more than two or three hours a day, and he was always gone by noon. He would come in between nine and ten in the morning, and I would get him a cup of coffee—black. The first thing he would do is go to his closet and put his hat away—he always wore a hat; a felt hat in the fall and winter, and a straw hat in the spring and summer. Then he would go and sit at his desk, where I would already have a stack of stuff, including mail, waiting for him on the corner.

Much of what was there was stuff that people had sent in for him to autograph, such as his books or photos of him. I would ask him if he felt like autographing that day, and would then tell him of any special instructions accompanying any of the autograph requests. There were often a few golf balls included in the things to be autographed, even though they were difficult for him to sign. He would sign them by opening the middle drawer in his desk and use a corner of the drawer to anchor the ball while he signed it. Sometimes, too, there would be people who would show up wanting to have their pictures taken with him. There were also times I would take dictation for him and that went quite quickly because he seemed to already know exactly what he wanted to say. I think there were even times that he had already written the text down (in longhand) before he would dictate it to me.

He did love the factory. He loved to go back there and watch what was going on, and I'm sure he made some remarks to people while back there. He just wanted to know what was going on. There was absolutely no ego in the man. He was not a highly educated person, and I think he was a sort of self-conscious person because of that. But he was a true gentleman from the word go—he never said any harsh words to or in front of the ladies, but I guess there were some times he really cut up some men.

—⚹—

*Hogan's last day at his Fort Worth office was **Doxie Williams**'s most memorable there. The occasion was the closure of the Hogan Company's Fort Worth headquarters after it was sold to AMF, Inc., and moved (in 1993) to Richmond, Virginia:*

It was the Friday preceding the Memorial Day weekend, and we were the last ones there to turn off the lights and leave the building. Movers were coming that afternoon, and I had been packing things and labeling them, getting things ready for the movers. I reminded him that we would be moving to our new offices the following Tuesday, after the three-day weekend. I walked him to his private entrance as I had always done, as he had a separate door that led right out to where his car was parked on the side. This time, as I was seeing him out, he stepped out the door and then he turned around, touched an index finger to his mouth, and put his finger on the door handle like he was kissing it good-bye. That nearly brought me to tears. He had this really pitiful look on his face because I know he really loved that place. It really broke his heart to be moving out of it.

For as long as the Hogan Company was based in Fort Worth, Hogan would dutifully come to his office every morning for a couple of hours, even long after he had sold the company. Hogan's managerial style was anything but warm or laissez-faire. **Jerry Austry** *was among those who walked on eggshells around Hogan. Austry came to the Hogan Company from Wilson Sporting Goods in 1984, and was promoted to president less than a year later after Roger Corbett was fired from that position. Austry sums up his four-year tenure as president, which abruptly ended after the company was again sold, this time to a Japanese industrialist, Minoru Isutani:*

What I learned to do was to meet with him every morning after I took over as president to go over things with him and thus keep him in the loop. Before going to work for the Hogan Company, I had worked for Wilson Sporting Goods, and they had this image over there of how good the clubs were at Hogan, not knowing that the company really didn't have any manufacturing controls for things such as swing weights and all that other stuff. When I got to the Hogan Company, they were losing market share, and I told Hogan it was because people were thinking that our clubs were too good for them. I told him we needed to convince people that we could make the Cadillac of pickups. With that, I started soliciting his input in the direction we were heading, and after that we got along much better. I wish I had made notes during our meetings because I met with him an hour a day every day for two years. But I never talked to him in the afternoon because by that time of the day he was out at Shady Oaks, having a "good afternoon" and being angry at the world. You never knew what anger would come spewing out of him.

Our losing market share opened the door for us to come up with a model golf club more suitable for Hogan's tastes. So we—engineers and manufacturers—all sat down, knowing that everyone those days was talking about getting clubs that had feel. Forged clubs were then perceived as the only ones that gave golfers feel. We were looking for a club that had the feel of the forge with the performance of a Ping, which by then was the standard of the golf-club industry. Ping was going crazy; its sales were out of sight. I went in to Mr. Hogan and said, "Here's where we're at. Our sales are disappearing, we're losing our position in the marketplace, and people are buying Pings. I need your help in going after Karsten Solheim." That did the trick, and we pushed ahead on developing the Edge clubs.

Ben would hit clubs that were in development and tell us what he liked and what he didn't like. A couple of times, he just tossed the clubs back at me and said they were crap. After about two or three months of this, I asked him what he wanted to do. After all, he had pride of authorship. I was always asking him for suggestions and asking him to support his objections. I would say,

"You're a master designer and I need your help in understanding why this isn't any good so I can translate this into language that consumers will understand." This way, he didn't get ticked at me because he knew I was looking for answers and he respected that.

———

Austry was surprised when he was let go in late 1988, in part because of the timing—the Edge clubs having just had a successful launch, and in part because he had lost an ally:

While we were introducing the Edge I came back from a vacation in Hawaii and found out I was being let go. So instead of going to the PGA Merchandise Show in early '89 to bask in our new success, I went there to network, looking for a new job. What happened was that the Hogan Company was being bought by a Japanese firm for $58 million, and they wanted to put their own management team in place.

The thing that hurt me the most was when I went to see Mr. Hogan asking for his help after the company had been sold. I really thought he would help me because some time back he had stood up at a sales meeting and said, "I never had a son, but if I had had one, I would have wanted him to be like Jerry." But when I went in there to talk to him about helping me out, the silence was deafening. He wasn't going to help me, so all I left with was some severance. As this was going on, I had remembered the time I had heard him say that if ever the Japanese bought the company, he would walk away. They would still own his name, but he would have no part of the company. So much for that. He didn't go to bat for me and that produced an open wound for me.

━━◆━━

Veteran tour golfer **John Jacobs** *praises the Hogan product, but not its promotion:*

Hogan clubs are a good club. The problem with Ben was that he kept it small, like a family-type operation, and he didn't take it to the worldwide level that you really need to do to make a lot of money. But he made as good a product as anybody. He probably just didn't promote it the way he should have to make a lot of money, but his product was fine.

━━◆━━

Tommy Jacobs, *John's brother, respected Hogan's ability to evaluate golf clubs, even if he didn't always get the answer he wanted:*

There was a time back in the 1960s when I was working for a company in Los Angeles that was producing a forerunner of the aluminum shafts. I had called Ben up and asked him if he would do some testing of the new shafts. I sent him some shafts but never heard back from him. Finally, later, I was playing in a tournament at Doral down in Miami, and I ran into Ben walking out of the locker room. I asked him about the shafts I had sent him, and he didn't say a word. All he did was shake his head and walk away. That was just Ben, and I knew him pretty well.

━━◆━━

Like many tour golfers of his generation, Hogan garnered ample experience as a club pro, back in the days when golf had a winter season, not a Silly Season, and tour pros hooked up in the off-season with prominent clubs looking for a prominent host pro. Hogan's club-pro experience included stints at Tamarisk Golf Club in Rancho Mirage, California. Hogan never forgot his pro-shop roots and would sometimes engage Shady Oaks head pro **Mike Wright** *in some businesslike shoptalk:*

I learned when I talked to him not to shoot from the hip. If I would ask a question, it needed to be thought through, and there should be a definite reason for asking it. And he was very, very smart. He asked me questions before I got this job—not in an interview, but just in general conversation about things like inventory levels of golf shops, turn ratios of inventory, sales per square footage, sales per round, margin of profit, methods of maintaining inventory—stuff like that. One day we talked in the golf shop for two hours about the golf business and the business of being a club pro and how you tie all things together. This was when I was an assistant. I always felt that was an important part of this job. He knew a lot about being a club pro. Teaching. Trying to communicate with people. He watched me teach and he admired people who could communicate verbally and influence other people with their golf.

—

Hogan had some hits and some misses in the oil business, but when the ledger book weighed earnings against losses, Hogan came out well ahead, as **Tex Moncrief** *points out:*

People would bring Ben deals every once in a while. He got into a deal up in Kansas and got a well that is still producing and makes several thousand dollars a month. He also filed some stuff in central west Texas, where he had some fellow that had brought the deal operating it but he was double-charging Ben. Hell, he was charging him to operate it and charging him for supervision. When Ben got sick he asked me, as Valerie did, about the cost of it. When I got their bills and all that, I looked at it and I said, "Well, this is ridiculous." I had a friend out there, an oil operator, who took a look at it. Sure enough, it was going on, but we cleaned it all up. Ben did all right. He made some pretty good money in the oil business.

His brother, Royal Hogan, would get into an oil deal every once in a while with us or hear us talking about an oil deal. We played golf with Royal Hogan all the time. He was a very good amateur and a couple years older than Ben. Royal would be playing golf with us and hear us talking about a deal, and he would say, "Could I have some of that?" Royal did very well in the oil business. Ben did have some oil dealings with a fellow named M. O. Rife Jr., and M. O. was quite a character. His dad worked for Gulf, and M. O. had a drilling company and he had a drilling come in. And M. O. had some properties with Ben, and some of them were up in north Texas, around Wichita Falls. They also had a few properties and a little well or two out in west Texas. They went on a trip one time, Ben with M. O., and they went around to their properties out in west Texas, and this may even have been as far out as Lea County, New Mexico. They had this well that they had drilled and it wasn't doing any good. M. O. walked around there and tried to kick a pipe sticking up—the casing or the drill pipe—something. Anyway, he kind of kicked that thing and said, "You no good son of a gun," and he picked up a piece of loose pipe that was sitting on the derrick floor and dropped it down the pipe.' Ben said, "M. O., what are you doing?" And ole M. O. said, "Oh, that's a no-good-sorry-son-of-a-gun well." They decided to split their properties. Ben had taken all he could stand of M. O. So Ben said, "Well, M. O., let's split this up. I'll take the west Texas stuff and you take the north Texas stuff." And M. O. says, "That's fine with me." That's what they did, and everything that Ben got in west Texas turned out to be dry, but M. O. hit it pretty good in north Texas.

Engaging in the world of business sometimes means having to deal with lawsuits, and Hogan was no exception, as his attorney **Dee Kelly** *explains:*

As far as I know he was involved in only one lawsuit in his life, and that happened after he discharged an operator of some oil properties that he owned. He had employed the man to run his operations. Valerie thought that he was not treating Ben correctly, and she persuaded Ben to discharge him. Hogan won the lawsuit. However, Ben wasn't in real good health then. His memory was impaired. I'm not sure that at the time he fully understood what had been going on, but he had to rely on Valerie to help him to a certain extent. There were times that he was totally lucid, but he did have these periods where he had trouble recollecting things. She was sharp, and she and Ben were very conservative. They left a sizable estate. He planned it, and he did well. When Valerie passed away (in June 1999), she left $1 million each to (Fort Worth's) University Christian Church and the Cook Children's Medical Center. He and Valerie went to church regularly and they sat in the back pew. They lived a quiet life.

He was very pleasant. Many times I'd go to my locker room at Shady Oaks and find some golf balls, and he even gave me a set of golf clubs one time, which I really appreciated. And he had a set of woods designed for me. He was a very generous man, a very kind man. He was very, very easy to represent. When it came to understanding the law, he would want to know what the situation was and he would ask me my advice. Once I'd given it to him, he would follow it. I'll never forget one time I did something for him and didn't charge him anything, and he got on me about that.

---

*For a period of time during the 1990s, the Hogan Company headquarters was moved to Richmond, Virginia. It spent five years there until Spalding Sports Worldwide bought the company and moved its Ben Hogan custom-built operations back to Fort Worth in October 1998. Before Spalding bought, and brought, the Hogan Company back, **Marty Leonard** had put together a small group in an attempt to bring the company back to Fort Worth herself. Leonard explains:*

It was a very painful experience for the Hogans when the company was moved away from here (in 1993). They had to move their offices away from where they had been for all those years. I would love to have had that opportunity to buy the company, but I understand why it was sold to a company like Spalding. But I continued to have contact with the holding company and have gotten to know them, and we've tried to be helpful to them in terms of what we think would work best for the Hogan Company.

My father had been heavily involved with Hogan and the company and investing in it, and he made some money out of it. So of course I had that interest. I didn't have a sophisticated business operation put together, but there were three of us, including designer Tom Stites, who had his own company and had some great ideas about clubs. We made an offer, and it was kind of exciting to give it a try. The thing you need to be careful about is to not make the Hogan Company something that it couldn't be. It was a niche company. It's not a club that's going to appeal to the masses and it can't be a Callaway or whatever. I think Spalding is going about it the right way and I am hopeful that they will be successful with it. Whether I could have made it work or not, I don't know.

Marty Leonard *had long been aware of Hogan's business acumen. She wasn't privy to business discussions between her father and Hogan, but she knew enough about her father to know how Hogan's business persona was being shaped:*

Daddy didn't talk about business at home. We had four girls and no boys, and somehow that's just not something any of us ever got very much involved in. But I know he was very interested and involved from an investor stand-point and probably giving Ben advice, certainly not from a golf club design standpoint, but with his club business, with Ben's business and stuff.

The impression I get is that Hogan really tried to acquire a lot of knowledge. He was a good businessman. And that doesn't always go with the other, but he was a smart businessman. I can remember my father acknowl-edging that he was a pretty good businessman himself, so he would know. You don't just start a golf-equipment manufacturing company and start being successful just because of a name. There's a lot of names that have tried and struggled. He just knew how to go about it and he was probably careful. Daddy got him involved in some other business ventures, too. He had a good sense about how to run a business and how to make good business deals. He was very much involved, and we all knew he was a perfectionist. That carried over into a lot of things he did. The way he lived, the way he dressed. And he worked hard. My guess is he worked at his business just like he did his golf game, and that's the reason he did well.

———

Gene Smyers, a Fort Worth insurance executive and one of Hogan's trusted friends and advisors, said that the estate Hogan left behind was much greater than what he had earned as a tour golfer:

Ben protected his assets. He was concerned about insur-ance. He had been involved in that terrible accident, and he would comment that if that had happened today the name of that bus company would have been "the Hogan Bus Company" rather than Greyhound Bus. But Ben amassed an estate that is probably significantly greater than most people ever have thought of. That's surprising in light of the fact that in Hogan's golf career he won only about $300,000.

For the home that he built in Fort Worth, they made the bricks on-site and I used to go up to watch the house being built with Ben's brother-in-law. I have no idea how many fireplaces they built before there was one that was complete. But that was Ben—he was the same way about golf clubs. Probably the greatest story about how exacting he was, was when the Hogan Company came out with its first set of clubs to be sold through the pro shops. They got the clubs out, and Ben, after he hit balls with them and looked at the clubs, said he was totally dissatisfied and called them all in. You could drive to the Hogan plant and you could see all those clubs stored in a loft. I won't say Ben was in trouble financially at the time, but the Hogan Company was, and his partners were reluctant to put any more money into it. So, in order to enable Hogan to retool, redesign, and remanufacture, Marvin Leonard invested in the Hogan Company. They retooled and went on to produce the premier golf club in the industry. If Mr. Leonard hadn't come in with fresh capital, it would have been gone. I heard the banks weren't receptive to it. I think he had possibly gone to the banks seeking funding for the retooling and so forth, but at that point he had nothing really to sell but his name.

Sportswriter-author **Dan Jenkins** *probably knew Hogan better than any other media-type, and that meant knowing that as astute as Hogan was at business, his name was never for sale. Here's an excerpt from an essay Jenkins wrote for the book* The Hogan Mystique *that explains Hogan's desire to keep his name pure:*

Hogan's name . . . was something he valued greatly and was very protective of. Unlike today's touring pros, he would never have rented it out to any logo that came down the fairway dressed like a kitchen appliance, compact car, or fast-food franchise.

He had numerous opportunities to put his name on everything from cupcakes to vacation resorts, but he saved it for the classy golf clubs he would eventually design and manufacture.

This pride in his name was instilled in him by his mother, long before there were golfing victories. He shared this with me one day back in the 1950s when we were sitting around Colonial Country Club, his home course at the time.

As I recall, Ben was talking about someone asking him to endorse something he regarded as unworthy of him—or any other human being. He said, "I've never forgotten what my mother told me when I was a boy. She said we might not be well off, but I was as good a person as anybody else in the world."

Then with a look, he added, "Your name is the most important thing you own. Don't ever do anything to disgrace it or cheapen it."[8]

Ben Hogan at age seventeen with his mother, Clara Hogan. (Photograph provided courtesy of Jacqueline Hogan Towery)

*Hogan was as relentless in business as he was in golf, and he always seemed to know which questions to ask, as Fort Worth geologist **Bob Wynne** can attest to:*

He was in the oil business—he was an oil operator and had some properties. He was the type of person who didn't get into something frivolously—he got into it in depth. When he found out I was a petroleum geologist, he would quiz me relentlessly. He knew a lot about certain parts of the science and was eager to learn more. I would enjoy talking to him and he obviously enjoyed talking to me. We became very close friends, and to be a close friend of Hogan's you had to be quiet. You just couldn't rattle on all the time or he would shut you out. He never talked about golf unless he wanted to. If he brought the subject of golf up, it was always very enlightening or amusing tales of his career experiences. I was in the Nineteenth Hole at Shady Oaks quite often. No one sat in Hogan's chair, and everyone knew which one it was.

Hogan didn't suffer fools or frivolous talk, and I think this was part of the reason he was misunderstood. If you had something to say and knew what you were talking about, he couldn't be nicer. I didn't know him in the prime of his career, but as I got to know him and understand him, I thought he was a great guy. I was once asked what he would have done if he hadn't been a golfer, and I said anything he wanted to do. Anything he did he was the best at. One story was that he was the best pool player in town when he was younger. Not only was he a great athlete, he was smart, too. For instance, there was a (oil) discovery west of town. No one could figure out what had happened—it wasn't very deep. Some reports mentioned that it might have been a granite intrusion that created the anomalous situation. He started reading about it, and one day he said, "Bob, tell me what you know about granite."

I said, "In what regard, Mr. Hogan?"

"Well, what is *basement*?"

"Well," I said, "when they're talking about basement, they're talking about granite, and when you drill through to the basement, you usually stop."

And he said, "Well, why do you stop?"

And I said, "It's just very difficult to drill through, and most of the time when you get there, there aren't going to be any sediments that could contain hydrocarbons below the granite."

"Well, why is that? How do you know? Have you ever drilled through it?"

"No sir, down where I drill, we don't ever get that far. But out in west Texas where they do, that's just about as far as they can go."

"I don't believe that."

"Well, there are times when you have a sill; you can drill through that sill if it's not too thick, and reach sediments again."

He said, "Okay, that's what I was asking about. I think it probably went through out there and got into a reservoir that kept producing oil."

He didn't give up when he wanted to know the answer. You just couldn't put him off, and that was true in everything, especially golf.

NOTES

1. Byron Nelson, *How I Played the Game* (Dallas: Taylor Publishing, 1993), 229.

2. Ben Crenshaw, "The Hawk," in *The Hogan Mystique* (Greenwich, Conn.: The American Golfer, 1994), 29.

3. Arnold Palmer, with James Dodson, *A Golfer's Life* (New York: The Ballantine Publishing Group, 1999), 138–39.

4. Herbert Warren Wind, "Hogan: On the Eve of Olympic, 1955," reprinted in *Herbert Warren Wind's Golf Book* (New York: Simon and Schuster, 1971), 78.

5. Palmer and Dodson, *A Golfer's Life*, 120–21.

6. Nelson, *How I Played the Game*, 20–21.

7. Jack Whitaker, *Preferred Lies and Other Tales* (New York: Simon and Schuster, 1998), 179–80.

8. Dan Jenkins, "Hogan His Ownself," in *The Hogan Mystique*, 38.

INDEX

ABOUT THE AUTHOR

Mike Towle is a veteran sportswriter and author whose previous books include *True Champions* and *The Ultimate Golf Trivia Book*. A former newspaper reporter, he has covered golf for the *Fort Worth Star-Telegram* and *The National*. He has also written numerous articles for *Golf World, Golf Shop Operations, Golf Journal,* and *Golf Illustrated* magazines. Towle is president and publisher of TowleHouse Publishing Company, based in Nashville, Tennessee, where he lives with his wife, Holley, and their son, Andrew.

Printed in the USA
CPSIA information can be obtained
at www.ICGtesting.com
JSHW021523110324
58997JS00004B/198

9 781630 269937